Drew Provan

Public Speaking

In easy steps is an imprint of In Easy Steps Limited
Southfield Road · Southam
Warwickshire CV47 0FB · United Kingdom
www.ineasysteps.com

Notice of Liability
Every effort has been made to ensure that this book contains accurate and current information. However, In Easy Steps Limited and the author shall not be liable for any loss or damage suffered by readers as a result of any information contained herein.

Trademarks
All trademarks are acknowledged as belonging to their respective companies.

Printed and bound in the United Kingdom

ISBN 978-1-84078-374-2

Contents

4 Practice Makes Perfect 61

5 Props May Help 73

6 Getting Ready For the Big Day 87

7 Looking the Part 101

8 Delivery 115

9 Taking Questions 131

10 Speaking Occasions 141

11 Further Resources 173

Index 187

1 Why Speak?

Public speaking is not a natural ability for most of us. The ability to put together a coherent speech and deliver this with authority is a great life skill, both in your professional and personal life.

What's the Big Deal?

Why bother? "*I don't want to do this. It's too difficult.*" Yes it is – speaking in public is not easy. Some people make it *look* easy but it takes much planning and practice to make it look easy.

Public speaking is a great skill to have both personally and professionally. If you have mastered it, and are comfortable speaking to an audience, then you should congratulate yourself. Most people dread this limelight and would rather do anything than stand up in public and talk to friends, colleagues or peers. Why? Because public speaking is scary.

The anxiety often starts days or weeks before the event and results in poor sleep and loss of appetite for many (not to mention the effect it can have on your gut!) The speaking engagement gets blown out of all proportion and people always fear the worst! I am not sure what the "worst" is, but I have seen very few people have a really bad time presenting a speech. Nonetheless, people build the event up into something gargantuan that becomes all-consuming. The reality is very different, and people get up, deliver their speech and think later "That wasn't so bad!" So, what are the advantages to being able to speak in public?

Career

Most jobs nowadays involve some public speaking. Certainly in business, education, medicine, law, sciences and the arts you will be called on to speak. The better you speak, the more you will be asked to speak and

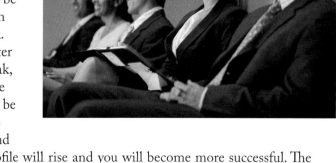

your profile will rise and you will become more successful. The business will also become more successful, so your employer will be happy.

Social

It is a great advantage to be able to get up at a wedding or leaving party and say a few words without falling apart. Being able to do this is a real ego boost and you will be appreciated by the group to whom you are speaking.

So public speaking *is* a big deal – it is important to you personally, as well as your organization. Yes, it may be tough at times, but this skill is one well worth mastering since it will open up many doors which might otherwise remain closed. The key features of a good public speaker are self-confidence and mastery of your material. Once you have these you should be comfortable giving speeches to a handful of people or audiences of 1,000 or more.

Confidence

You may already be a confident person but you could raise this to the next level through learning to present well, and get your point across in a concise and clear manner. If you tend to steer clear of situations that put you in the spotlight, you will learn to overcome this fear. By tackling Question & Answer sessions after a presentation you will no longer stumble over your arguments during one-on-one discussions.

So, in its narrowest sense, learning to speak in public helps you inform and entertain, and in the broadest sense it can help you become stronger, sharper and more confident.

Hot tip

Great speakers are not born. They have worked hard to get where they are. With determination and practice you can raise your game to a much higher level.

Good Speakers Are Not Born

Professional speakers are everywhere, on the TV, radio and the Internet. They make it look easy. No matter which subject they are presenting they make it sound interesting. Yet if you attend an internal meeting at work the presenter generally makes the topic sound dull, even when they know the subject well. The same is true of professional conferences. The Chairmen usually fail to get the audience excited, introduce the speakers in a lazy way and the talks themselves are often boring.

The real pros (those on TV, radio and other media) have been trained to present the way they do. They have no innate gift that makes them so interesting. The misconception, however, is that these skills are complex. The opposite is true – with a little effort, planning and practice we can all deliver good speeches. But few of us really commit the time or effort, and we tend to emulate our peers and subject them to half-hearted attempts that are, well, boring.

Some natural talent and enthusiasm does help, though. For example, if you are a natural extrovert and enjoy the limelight then standing up in front of a group of people will not be as daunting as it would be for someone who is shy. Nonetheless, even the most shy individuals can master the art of powerful presentation provided some effort is put in during the early stages.

Examples of inspirational speakers

Barak Obama is a current example of someone who knows how to play to the crowd. His timing is excellent. He talks to thousands of people yet makes it feel intimate, as if he is only talking to you. He has passion and enthusiasm which helps get his message through clearly. Look at the way he works the crowd and scans the arena, "touching" each person.

Why are they inspirational?

- They *talk* to us rather than lecture at us

- They make it look effortless

- We can truly *identify* with what they are saying

- The content has real *relevance* to us

- They make us think more about ourselves, our actions, and they can *change* the way we think and act

Everyone Can Improve

Try not to dwell on negative experiences associated with previous presentations or speeches. This creates a downward spiral – maybe your last speech did not go well, the audience seemed bored so you fear that the next one will probably fail too. Don't allow negative thoughts or feedback to affect your next speech. This represents a fresh opportunity to shine and, with more effort and planning, the next one will be better.

So much of our professional and personal life benefits from achieving success through public speaking that it is really worth the effort to work hard at this and achieve maximum impact.

Beware

Do not dwell on bad speaking experiences. Learn from them and move on.

Put the speaking experience to good use

Each time you give a talk, speech, sermon or lecture you learn more about your subject and yourself. You gain experience in learning how to pace yourself, improve your timing so you seldom overrun your slot, you also learn how to construct better slides or other audiovisuals. Your degree of anxiety will lessen the more you put yourself in the hot seat – it is *impossible* to be very anxious if you regularly speak in public. Even the most skeptical people realize that they are improving so they feel less uptight about speaking. Each time you give a talk, jot down a few notes on what went well and what went badly. Next time you are asked to give a speech, try to improve on the weak areas.

Don't forget

With practice and experience your anxiety level will diminish. It is impossible to remain highly anxious if you speak in public regularly.

Communication is Critical

Hot tip

The ability to speak well will set you apart from other candidates if you are competing in the job market.

Public speaking skills may help you secure that job!

The job market is tough and there are usually several people competing for the same post. Everyone will be well qualified and interviewers will be looking for key skills that will help them select the best candidate for the job.

It is common for interviewees to be asked to give a short presentation before the main interview begins. The presentation title is often broad in order to see what critical information the candidates can find, and test their skills in finding faults with current strategies, or seeing how good they are at highlighting ways of improving sales, company image, team morale, and other "weaknesses". Interviews are stressful at the best of times, but if you have to deliver a speech before the interview starts this adds to the pressure considerably. If you present your material well, and handle the questions during the speech, you will have established yourself as someone who can handle pressure without falling apart. One advantage of the pre-interview presentation is that your nerves will calm down after the presentation which should make the interview proper that little bit easier.

Use public speaking to help you sell

The business world is a tough place. All companies, whether financial, manufacturing, education or medicine, need to have a presence and visibility. Organizations need spokespeople – individuals who can think fast on their feet, can talk to the media and deliver presentations well, with total clarity and focus. If you have these skills you will become a real asset to your company and will reap the rewards.

Use public speaking to help you persuade

Maybe you have faulty goods and want to complain about them, or want to argue against an unfair parking fine? Generally we just back down and pay up. But if you were better able to present your case and argue you might be better off discussing your dissatisfaction with the shop or parking authority. This often takes nerve, and the skills acquired through learning to project yourself during public speeches can be used for just this very thing!

Preparation Takes Weeks

The speech is only the tip of the iceberg

Public speaking is always viewed as the actual pitch itself, where the speaker stands up on a stage or behind a microphone and delivers his or her message. But this is just the tip of the iceberg – the final part of a long process. Trust me, this is the easier part, in a way.

Most of the work lies underneath. Before getting up to give that speech you will have had to weigh up the pros and cons of speaking and accept the invitation. You will have spent many hours researching the topic area and made notes on paper or using a PC.

You will then need to organize your thoughts and your notes in order to make sure your key messages are clear. Your slides or notes will have to be refined so that they flow in a logical order ending up with a conclusion that encapsulates all that you have said, while driving home the key messages. You will have practiced extensively, alone and to colleagues to make sure the content of your speech makes sense.

All of this will take weeks if you are to do it well. So the actual delivery of the speech may only take 30 minutes but if your preparation has been extensive and focused your speech will be clear, focused and will leave the audience with a strong impression of you, and your key points.

The Audience

Put yourself in the audience's seat

While you are thinking through the content of your speech, consider what *you* would like to hear if you were in the audience rather than on the podium. What style would you find interesting? Or boring? We have already looked at what makes some speakers inspirational so that should provide some clues.

Based on the title of your presentation, what would you expect to hear from the presenter? What would you *not* want to listen to? As an audience member, why might you be there at all? What is your role? Expert? Novice?

One of the first things you must get right is knowing how to pitch to *this* audience. Who are they, what do they know about the subject matter and what will they expect from your talk? If you get this right, the audience will be appreciative. If you get this wrong (for example a dumbed down speech to people with extensive knowledge of the topic) the audience will be bored (at best) or hostile (at worst).

Whoever invited you to give this speech will have a pretty good idea of what is expected of you. So, if you are not completely clear about what they want from you – ask! It does no harm to clarify this well before you start to research the topic. You may save many wasted hours of frustration if you can get this sorted right at the beginning.

Beware

You must find out who the audience is and what they expect to hear from you. Tell them what they want to hear not what you want them to hear.

14

Speaking Skills Can Help

The ability to speak in public is a major asset, in any career. There are many jobs where regular public speaking is not required, but this skill goes way beyond the delivery of a "lecture" or similar style of speech. Most of us have face-to-face contact with senior management to review our job plans, for appraisals, to monitor progress of a project or role. If you can talk to small groups in a calm and determined manner this will help your seniors understand how the project is progressing, or your role in their business. If you are seeking promotion you can plan your speech well before you meet them and put your case to them in a clear way and secure the promotion you deserve. On the other hand, if you tend to avoid conflict and exposure within your organization you will not be "seen" and quite possibly you will not secure the promotion or recognition. Presenting to peers or seniors can be daunting for many people, and just as frightening as standing up on a stage speaking at a conference. By developing good strategies, and with planning, you will be able to stand up and be counted.

A good grasp of public speaking is useful for:

- Job interviews
- Promotion interviews
- Asking your bank manager for a loan
- Internal presentations to your team at work
- National or international conferences
- Chairing committee meetings
- Panels or advisory board meetings
- Debates
- Web-based presentations
- Leaving parties
- Weddings
- Funerals
- Impromptu speeches
- Other social gatherings

Hot tip

Developing the skills of public speaking will help you in your personal life as well as your professional career.

What Makes a Good Speaker?

As with all aspects of life, there are good and bad speakers. Those whom we rate highly are interesting to listen to. They talk *to* us, not *at* us, and at our level. They tend to remain on message throughout (although diversions are interesting!) They vary the pitch of their speech and avoid speaking in a monotone. They often use gestures involving their faces, arms, hands or whole body. Very often they will move around the stage or the room looking at different groups within the audience. They avoid turning their backs on us even if they are presenting visual material. They make us feel included in the discussion, almost like a one-on-one discussion, even if the audience is large.

Great speakers avoid the over-use of technical terms just for the sake of it, and speak in a natural manner which is very easy to understand. They may use humor but they will avoid "jokes". They would never use racist or sexist material unless they are stand-up comedians but we are not talking about that type of presentation here.

Within the workplace, a good public speaker can be inspirational, making us feel more committed to the company or our role within the organization. This is critical if you are managing staff or trying to influence behavior.

People who are skilled in public speaking can help us learn complex concepts without overburdening us with details. Most importantly of all, after we have listened to a skilled speaker we will be able to recall the key messages long after the event since they will have used techniques throughout their speech to ensure there are only a few key messages and they will have been repeated throughout the speech and again at the end.

Features of a good speaker, in a nutshell

- Has a real *understanding* of the subject area

- Someone who is *passionate* about this

- Uses *simple language* to explain even the most complex of concepts

- Tells a *great story*, often with a sense of theater

- Has *polish* and style, can *connect* with the audience and hold their attention for however long the speech takes

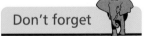

Don't forget

Good speakers are passionate in what they do. They tell a great story and can hold the audience's attention.

What Makes a Bad Speaker?

Unfortunately, we have all listened to many bad speakers in our time. Often they will start late and have a slide deck with material that has been used for other similar speeches. They are often very busy people who therefore do not have enough free time to tailor their speeches to individual audiences. They may not worry too much about the actual delivery style and end up talking in a monotonous manner that becomes boring after a while. Their style is often not individual and feels less like a conversation.

Features of a bad speaker
- May not know the subject as well as they would like you to think

- They may be passionate but it does not show. Their delivery style is boring and monotonous

- They try to impress by having their slides crammed with huge amounts of bulleted text lists and irrelevant graphics

- Their sense of theater is missing and their timing is poor

- Complex areas are not well explained

- They lack polish, and often just recycle old talks

- As a result they fail to persuade, educate or motivate

Beware

A lack of passion and slides crammed with unnecessary detail will result in a lack-luster pitch. You will bore the audience.

Choosing the Topic

The title of your talk is usually designed by one of the organizers of the session. It may be very tight such as *"Xenopus oocyte cAMP-dependent protein kinases before and during progesterone-induced maturation"* which leaves little to the imagination and gives the speaker a very limited remit or *"Control of cell division in mammalian cells"* which is very broad – here the speaker could talk about kangaroos or humans and can choose which aspects to discuss.

Maybe you don't like the title of the talk which they have provided. In this case you should talk to the organizers and see if you can modify the title, perhaps making it broader so that you can develop the theme the way you want, and not be forced to talk about something which you are not interested in.

Broad titles are best

As outlined above, try to keep the title of your talk as broad as possible. This gives you much more flexibility when it comes to writing the speech. Use phrases like *"Advances in ..."*, *"Developments in ..."*, *"Update on ..."*, or *"Review of ..."* since these essentially allow you to talk about anything you want. This has the advantage that if something crops up between now and your speech you can add it in without the content looking out of place. But do remember to discuss this with the people who have invited you to talk otherwise they might have a specific topic in mind, and if you change it they may be upset.

Hot tip

Try to choose the topic to suit you. If you are not happy with the suggested title, ask to have it changed to something more suitable for you.

Are You Qualified?

Flattery will get you everywhere

It is always flattering being asked to give a talk. In fact, the organizers know this and will make the invite so appealing you will hardly be able to refuse! They will use terms like *"As a recognized expert in the field… the committee would be honored if you would consider giving a lecture on…"*. One of the recent invites I have received was: *"Company X will organize a satellite symposium on product Y during this edition on Friday 09/01/09. Our colleagues from the European affiliate, Fred Bloggs and from the UK John Doe have recommended you as an expert and as an eventual speaker. We would be honored if you could give a presentation on this topic. Could you please let us know if you are interested and if this date suits you?"*

Flattering though invites may be, you should take a deep breath and look beyond the kind words. Are you *really* well-placed to talk about this? You may know a little but if this is an expert audience might they not expect something more than you can deliver? Sure, you can do some research but you also have a day job, and achieving the level required may not be possible.

Sleep on it

Do not answer the invitation straight away. Give it some serious thought and if you still feel you want to accept then do so. Check your diary – how many other talks are you giving? Can you really manage to squeeze another one in?

If you are *really* sure you have the knowledge required to pull this off then by all means accept the invitation (provided you really are clear what is expected and who the audience will be). But if you feel that maybe you are not up to it, try to suggest an alternative speaker. Usually we can think of colleagues who have a better working knowledge of certain aspects of the topic or organization. These people would be better to deliver this speech than you. If this is the case, thank the organizers (you do want to be invited in the future!) and tell them that this is not your area of expertise. However, your colleague Jane Doe is a *real* expert and would be able to address the topic they have suggested. Provide them with her name, title, address and email address if possible. This makes it very easy for them to get in touch with her. It will also ensure that they think you're a nice person for being so helpful and they will keep your name on the invite list. Your colleague will be delighted to be asked and should return the favor!

Beware

You may be flattered to be asked to give a speech but do not agree if you are not qualified for the job. The audience will realize this and will be disappointed.

Is There Time to Prepare?

Do not underestimate the time required to plan a good speech. You may be asked to speak only for 20 minutes but the preparation time required may be many hours. This includes writing a rough draft of the speech on paper, doing the research from books or the Web, typing your speech using a word processor or slide program such as PowerPoint. After this, you will need to go over your speech many times, adding and deleting items, checking the timing to make sure you can deliver the presentation within the time allotted to you.

Another time-consuming part of the task is practicing your speech. Simply writing it out and reading it over is not sufficient since you will skim over the text and assume the delivery in public will be as easy. This is not the case, and there may be areas where you stumble, or use words that are difficult to say, or there may be concepts that are difficult, requiring you to slow down to a crawl when you actually deliver the speech.

Checklist:

- What kind of speech are you making?
- Is it part of a conference?
- Are there any cultural or language issues?
- Clarify the title of your speech and what they expect you to include?
- Are there any areas they would prefer you avoid discussing?
- Are you there to entertain? Inform? Influence their behavior?
- Who is the audience? How many will be there?
- What do they know about the subject area? Are they experts?
- Is this part of a panel symposium?
- How many speakers are there?
- What are the titles of their presentations?
- Are you taking questions after your speech or during the presentation?
- Is there a Chairman? Who is it?

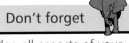

Don't forget

Plan all aspects of your speech to the last detail. Find out everything you can about the topic, the audience, format of the session, the titles of your co-presenters' speeches. After this you can start work on your own talk.

Strategy

If you have accepted the invitation to give a speech or presentation make yourself a checklist of things you need to do:

- Is the topic one that you can speak on? If you are not truly comfortable talking on this subject say so – early. Allow them time to find an alternative speaker

- Check your diary for availability. Are you free on the day of the speech? Is there any traveling to the venue?

- Is it outside your home country? If so, work out when you need to travel (the day before?) and that you are free on the days either side of the event

- Do you need to provide cover for your work when you are away from base?

- Check with your line manager that you can have the time off to attend the event

- Check title, venue, time allocated for speech

- If part of a conference, do you need to register, or will the organizers do this on your behalf?

- Will they book the plane, train or other transport?

- What is the format of the speech?

- Are they expecting you to use visuals such as PowerPoint?

- Do they require these in advance of the meeting?

- Do you need to take a laptop or can you use theirs?

- Is there a rehearsal before the event? Many conference organizers use this, especially corporate satellite sessions (this is to make sure you are not saying anything off-message!)

- How much time do you have to prepare your speech? You will need time to research, write, refine then practice (this may require four weeks or more depending on the topic)

Summary

- Being able to express yourself and convey your ideas clearly is critical in today's job market, where there is intense competition for jobs and promotion

- Public speaking is definitely a big deal. Being able to speak well, and engage an audience is a highly valuable transferable skill. If you can achieve this you will become an asset to your organization and you will enhance your own career prospects

- Attaining these skills takes time and practice. Natural speakers are not born. Instead, they work hard at perfecting their techniques so that when they get up to speak they are totally in control, are engaging and entertaining. The best public speakers can inspire us to work better, buy their goods and adopt their philosophy

- Even if you are not a great public speaker at present, you can work on your techniques and raise the level of your performances. This will boost your confidence allowing you to further improve on your delivery

- Do not underestimate the time it takes to craft a good speech. Delivering a 20 minute pitch may take you 4 weeks *or more* of work – make sure you have the time to commit to this before you accept the invitation

- Think about the audience and what they need as you write the speech. This is about them – not you. What would you most want to hear about if you were in their place?

- If this is a business meeting or academic conference make sure the topic is one you can talk about with confidence. If you are giving a best man's speech at a wedding, or some other social function, you will have little choice about accepting

- If you feel unqualified to speak on a topic say so, and suggest an alternative speaker

- Make sure you have sufficient time and resource to take this on?

- Check with your work colleagues if you need someone to cover for you while you are away from base

2 Nervous? You Are Not Alone!

If you did not feel some anxiety before giving a speech you would be unusual. Some anxiety is natural and helps give you an edge. If your anxiety is extreme it will impair your performance. There are several strategies that can help you – and others which will not.

Fear of Public Speaking

Most people fear public speaking

Being asked to speak in public strikes fear into most people. Few of us are truly comfortable standing up in front of an audience and delivering a speech. Some (lucky) people only become mildly anxious when speaking in public but many of us are reduced to wrecks when placed in front of an audience. For people not used to public exposure like this it is truly a scary time.

Happily, most of this can be overcome, and the anxiety state can be channelled into something positive which will add to your performance rather than detract from it. We will discuss this in detail later.

Beware

The anxiety felt when thinking about public speaking comes from the feeling we need to be 100% perfect. This is unrealistic. Lower the bar and make life easier!

Ever since we were children at school, putting ourselves in the limelight by raising our hand to answer a question has been nerve-wracking. Why? Mainly this is caused by a fear of appearing foolish, asking a "dumb" question, or giving the wrong answer to a question and having everyone laugh at you.

The performance anxiety we feel when we make a speech even to a small group centers on the need to be 100% perfect. We want the words to come out right, the timing to be perfect and the message to be crystal clear. We worry about stumbling over words or concepts, or not being able to answer questions perfectly. But setting yourself up for 100% perfection is the worst thing to do since no-one is ever this good when they present! It would be a truly amazing public speaker who never made any mistakes. Yet this is what we see as the gold standard and expect it of ourselves.

If you watch the great presenters on TV or listen to them on the radio you will notice that even they get things wrong (and they are usually reading an autocue!) The difference is they don't fall apart or give up when they make a mistake. They just carry on as if nothing has happened. This is what amateur presenters such as us have to do if we make a mistake.

But even though we see our colleagues make mistakes during their speeches we forgive them. So why do we beat ourselves up when we do the same thing? It's as though there is some inner self which is always looking over our shoulder critically, marking down each and every mistake. In fact, this is probably how lots of us work, psychologically. Rather than concentrate on all that went well, we dwell on the one or two negatives, allowing this to overshadow our success.

There is a book called *The Inner Game of Tennis* written by W Timothy Gallwey (Pan Books). As the title suggests, it is intended to help tennis players improve their game. But the inner game of tennis is also played inside our heads with the two opposing views we have of our performance (albeit music, speeches, acting, sport, or whatever): the bits we do well and the fear of failure and dwelling on the negatives.

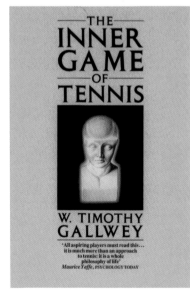

Anyone who has nagging doubts about their performances giving speeches or who wishes to banish the inner demons should read through this short book which has lots of strategies to help us become more confident speakers. If you *are* a tennis player you may raise that game, too!

Beware

We all have "inner voices" that hold us back, and impair our performance. You need to develop strategies to deal with doubt and self-ability.

Sources of Anxiety

What is it about public speaking that makes us so angst-ridden? Even fairly confident people are susceptible to an attack of nerves at the thought of getting up and speaking. The root causes appear to be:

Mastery of the content

You have been chosen to give this talk and whether this is an internal or external speech it is very likely that you will know more than anyone in the audience about the subject. Remember this. You have also carefully prepared the presentation, designed the slides around the content you feel is most suitable. You should literally know this backwards, and if you don't then you have not practiced enough. Complete familiarity with your subject matter is paramount to a successful presentation and, importantly, the Question & Answer session.

Audiovisuals good enough?

Are my slides good enough? Too much text? Too few illustrations? Generally, when we design slides we get to a stage where we are fairly happy with the content. However, as the speech day approaches we often worry that we have omitted vital information, or used poor or insufficient graphics. This is usually a stress reaction, and the likelihood is that you are feeling very nervous and your confidence is undermined. If you were happy with the slides earlier then the chances are they will be fine. Don't try adding content at a late stage since you will not be familiar with the content and risk over-filling your time slot.

All eyes are on you!

If you are a natural exhibitionist you will probably quite enjoy the attention that comes with speaking in public. Most people do not enjoy this and will avoid it if possible. All eyes will be on you. There is no getting away from this but confidence in what you are saying and a clear message will make you feel more assured. The audience wants to like you and they want the speech to be a success. Being center stage is something that you will simply have to bear and, with time, you will start to enjoy it.

Unknowns

How many people will be there? Are they experts? Will they be hostile or friendly? What will the room be like? Will I need to stand on a stage and use a microphone? These thoughts will recur

Hot tip

It may seem obvious, but mastery of the content of your speech will take you far, and you will feel much less stressed in the period leading up to your presentation.

until you reach the venue, but you can ask the organizers to give you some of these details. They will know what the set-up is, how many are likely to attend, and what their level of expertise is. This should help you reduce your anxiety. Once you get to the venue you will feel much calmer since you will then see the facilities.

Technical failure

Things can and do go wrong. Most of these are outside your control. Don't waste time worrying about things like failing laptops or projectors. You cannot influence these. You should, however, have multiple copies of your presentation on USB sticks and CD if possible, along with a printed copy of your slides or speech. This means that even if there is no electricity you will still be able to give your talk.

Performance failure

What if I bomb? Or forget my words? Of course this could happen but generally the worst that happens is that you forget the occasional detail or stumble over one or two words. Providing you correct the word and carry on the audience will not even notice. You are not trying to achieve 100% perfection – that would be totally unrealistic. Just do your best. They know you are only human and they just want to hear the content of your speech. They are not expecting a totally suave and slick presenter!

Hot tip

Technical glitches happen to all of us. It will happen to you, too, one day. Don't waste energy worrying about it. If it happens, you will deal with it.

27

The Audience is on Your Side

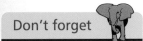

Don't forget

The audience is almost always on your side. They want you to succeed and they want to learn from you.

Even before you reach the venue, or as you sit at the front of the lecture room, you view it as an "us" and "them" situation, where the audience is intrinsically hostile, and out to get you. Does this make sense? No, it doesn't. Why would these people travel all the way here to see you falter or make a mistake? It's not likely. Instead, they have come with an open mind, usually hoping to learn something and hoping you can deliver it to them in the form of a speech. They are not expecting you to be perfect and the speech will be just as good even if you do make a few mistakes.

Get the audience in perspective

- They are likely to be your peers, friends, or others who want to hear what you have to say

- They are on your side

- They want you to succeed, not fail

- They are forgiving – up to a point. They will overlook small misdemeanors but will be less forgiving if you fail to engage, and consider their needs

- Not all 100% will give you positive feedback. Learn to live with this. You cannot please all of the people all of the time

- Beware of misconceptions ("*They know more than me*", "*They won't understand this*", "*They'll know this already*")

Why We Become Anxious

So it appears that the anxiety we feel stems from a need to be perfect.

We fear the audience and imagine them to be the enemy, even though we are in the audience ourselves quite frequently and we never feel like the enemy then! So why should they be against us?

We worry that the content of our material may not be good enough, or exhaustive enough, or current enough. But you know the field probably better than anyone in the audience so if you feel that what you have included is sufficient – then it is.

Maybe we don't really know enough about the topic? You might be starting to doubt your credentials – maybe some of the audience are more of an authority than you are?

But the organizers asked you and *not* them so that makes *you* the ideal person!

The Q&A session after the speech. What happens if you cannot answer the questions? This fear is very common but there are strategies for dealing with this and we will tackle this later in the book.

Other factors adding to anxiety

- The audience might laugh at you (not likely)

- Not finding the right word (so what?)

- Stumbling over words (just correct it and you'll be fine)

- We might disappoint the audience (we might, but most of them will be happy)

- We might not use the equipment properly, hit the back instead of forward button when using slides (this happens and isn't the end of the world, move on and get over it)

Biological Basis of Symptoms

Anxiety builds up as the event gets closer

Faced with a public appearance, most of us feel some anxiety, often starting many weeks before the main event. Initially the symptoms are mild but become more pronounced the nearer the big day becomes.

Typical symptoms include a generalized anxiety state, difficulty sleeping and maybe eating, loose stools, difficulty concentrating, fear that the material in the speech or slides is not good enough.

Nearer the date of the talk people often develop a tremor with shaky hands, butterflies, sweating, dry mouth, nausea, bounding pulse, and loss of concentration.

This won't hurt!

These symptoms we have are exactly like those associated with a visit to the dentist. Most of us remember this only too well with feelings of utter dread. We imagine the worst. It will hurt. It will be unpleasant. In the days before our appointment, out of the blue comes this feeling of doom! Then when we actually do go to the dentist there is no pain. The whole session is over before you know it. Why did you worry?

Adrenaline is the cause for most of our symptoms

All these symptoms and signs have a solid biological basis and we all go through pretty much the same if faced with a fearful situation. Nature has developed this response, which is known to biologists as the "flight or fight" response, because as part of our evolutionary development, when faced with something scary we have to make the decision between whether to face up to it and fight, or whether to run away. In order to fight well, blood is diverted away from less important organs like the gut, kidneys, and others. The blood is diverted instead to the muscles and brain. The heart rate increases in order to boost the cardiac output which maximizes blood flow to the muscles. This helps us in battle or, if we decide to flee, it makes sure we can run very fast. In fact, faced with this type of danger we can run much faster than if we were running for a bus where the anxiety level is much lower.

What is causing all this to happen? Adrenaline (also known as epinephrine), pure and simple. This hormone is released from the adrenal glands (these sit just above the kidneys) and bind to its receptors in a variety of tissues and exert their effects.

Hot tip

The anxiety symptoms we feel, and the outward display of "nerves" are caused by adrenaline. You can control this and use it to your advantage. It will give you an edge.

Overcome Anxiety

All performers feel anxious to a certain degree. This includes actors, musicians, chat show hosts, newsreaders, and of course people like you giving a speech at a wedding or conference. It would be very unusual to find someone who was totally at ease in this situation since we all have adrenaline flowing. So why do people in the public eye appear relaxed when they are on TV or the stage? They have learned to live with this feeling of heightened awareness and "stress" and they can channel their nerves positively. This improves their performance rather than worsening it.

Does public speaking get easier with time?

The answer has to be "yes". It does. If you give speeches regularly you will learn that even though you imagine that bad things could happen, nothing ever does and your body therefore adapts. It still sends out some adrenaline but less than before. You are able to eat and sleep better even right before the main event since you have subconsciously learned that you will be able to perform and nothing catastrophic will happen, even if your performance is not 100% perfect. It is common for people to wish for the day when they would not get stressed at all but if that were to happen the chances are your performance would lack a certain edge and would be less good than if you were a little bit anxious. The best actors and musicians have a certain (controlled) level of anxiety which improves their performance. So you should not aim to lose this, or be disappointed if you still feel anxious after working through the methods in this book.

Preparation is the best way to allay anxiety

The best method, in my opinion, for reducing anxiety associated with a public speech is to be totally prepared for the event. That means doing your homework, researching the topic, writing the plan for your speech on paper or using a word processor way before the event. If you are using slides these should also be written and refined well ahead of time. If you can do this, and you know your material well, your anxiety level will be much less than if you are frantically trying to write something a couple of days before the talk. Preparation is key. The same is true of music and acting – rehearsal and knowing our material makes us feel in control and much less anxious. We all have slight jitters before we go on, but that's fine. This is natural and to be expected. In fact, it's a bonus since it enhances the performance.

Hot tip

Solid preparation is a reliable way of reducing your anxiety level. Plan your speech carefully, rehearse extensively, and know your subject well.

Do Medicines Help Anxiety?

Quick fix

Is there a quick medicinal fix for anxiety? Yes and no. There are drugs that can help the acutely anxious person, but in general it is better to use natural solutions.

Sedatives

There are many of these. One example is the benzodiazepine group of drugs. These have been used for many years for acute anxiety. These induce sleepiness and a state of somnolence. They do reduce anxiety but are not good for people who wish to perform well. Unless you are totally climbing the walls and unable to function, steer clear of this type of drug.

Beta blockers

This includes propranolol (*Inderal* is one example). These drugs have been used by performance artists (musicians, actors, public speakers) for many years. They do *not* prevent anxiety but they *lessen the effects* of anxiety. They block some of the effects of adrenaline, and reduce the tremor and other effects associated with anxiety. Some musicians feel that they lose their "edge" if they take beta blockers and prefer to perform without them. Note, beta blockers may worsen many medical disorders such as asthma and heart failure and should never be taken unless specifically prescribed by a physician.

In general

Non-drug solutions are best, since no drug is without harmful effects for some people. Sure, the side effects are not commonly seen but they may occur so why take the risk?

It is better to develop your confidence through psychological means rather than through drugs. Learning what aspects of presentating make us scared gives us something to build on. This is a far better solution than reliance on pharmaceutical agents.

However, if you are rigid with fear and feel you simply cannot give a presentation but feel you must do so for your career, or whatever other reason, visit your family doctor and talk things through. See what options they suggest. If they feel that you are medically fit to take some of the anxiety reducing medicines then you might try these *as a short-term crutch*. Use the experience of speaking to make you stronger and reduce your reliance on medicines.

Beware

Prescribed drugs can sometimes help if you are highly anxious but, in general, psychological strategies are superior.

Strategies That May Help

There are lots of natural ways of relieving tension and stress before giving a speech. Taking a brisk walk helps loosen the muscles and gets rid of some tension that builds up. Breathing deeply in and out is also beneficial, as are head and neck exercises (turning your head slowly one way then the other a few times can release tension from the neck). Some people swear by stretching exercises in much the same way as athletes would use these.

Why not talk to the audience before the formal talk? It is always useful to be at the venue well before the start time. This gives you time to get used to the room, the seating arrangements, the stage (if there is one) and the equipment. Audience members will arrive as it gets nearer the time of the speech and you could wander among the seats or the coffee area and introduce yourself. That way, you will bond with at least some of them and they will no longer be "the enemy".

Desensitization

Many years ago, behavioral animal scientists looked at the way animals behave when subjected to noises. Initially they are fearful each time they hear the sound but eventually, since nothing untoward happened when the noise was made, they started to ignore it. They became desensitized.

The same thing happens when humans are subjected repeatedly to what appears to be an unpleasant situation. If nothing ever bad happens we start to relax and not worry about it. This will happen to you if you give many presentations. Your fear of the event will get less with each one until you have almost no fear at all.

Visualize success!

This may sound slightly corny but it does work. Imagine the applause at the end of your highly successful motivational speech. How great that would feel! Strive to achieve this by giving it your all. Start your presentation well (and quietly congratulate yourself) before moving on to the main part of your speech, then finally ending your talk with a great set of key messages. If you can imagine success you are half way there. You only have to get through the actual presentation to achieve this. Of course, you probably won't get a standing ovation but then, few people do, and it is generally only politicians or artists who manage to get people out of their seats. If you manage to get a warm applause and some good questions afterwards you are doing well!

Strategies That Seldom Help

People will often suggest strategies to help make you feel better before you take to the stage. "*Imagine the audience naked*" is often cited. Does this ever help anyone? I doubt it. "*Look for a friendly face in the audience*". If you have an audience of 200 you will end up grinning at one poor soul in the front row who will later develop a complex, wondering why you picked him or her out for special attention. What probably would be of help would be if you were to notice audience members nodding in agreement as you spoke. That would reassure you that some of what you were saying made sense. "*I am not very good at public speaking so I would like to apologize in advance…*". Never! Never ever apologize! Some people feel that by apologizing up-front they will somehow be excused if the talk goes wrong. This is not a good strategy and even if you feel like doing it – don't.

Dutch courage

Alcohol has been used by performers for decades because alcohol helps us to relax and alleviates many of the effects of adrenaline. The problem is it also makes it much more difficult to perform. If you give a speech under the influence of alcohol you risk delivering a poor speech and this will make you more nervous next time and you may drink alcohol again with similar results.

Many performers have become addicted to alcohol through using it in this way and this can lead to major alcohol dependence, cirrhosis and death. Alcohol is therefore *not* advisable as a crutch for people who need to speak in public on a regular basis.

On the other hand, if you are not in the public eye, but need to say a few words after a funeral and the others are drinking brandy or whisky, there is no reason why you should not have one too. It is the habitual use of alcohol that causes problems in those who need to perform on a regular basis.

Beware

Using alcohol to calm your nerves is not advisable. You may be more relaxed but your performance will suffer.

34

Strong Beginning and End

What is the worst part of any speech? It has to be the first couple of sentences you utter as soon as you take to the stage. People often worry about this part more than any other. Why? Well, it is probably at this point that you are at your most vulnerable. Your adrenaline rush will be at its highest and you will be closest to the "flight" part of the response. Once you get past the first couple of minutes your adrenaline level will start to drop and you will feel much better.

The opening few lines and slides, if you are using these, are absolutely critical to your talk. For this reason it pays to spend a considerable amount of your time working on these and getting them perfect.

Opening lines

Your title slide will be on the screen, with your name, role and organization, as well as the title of your presentation. "*Mr Chairman, thank you for inviting me to talk to you today. I am honored to be here to take part in this important session on widgets. My name is John Doe, and I am Vice President for Research & Development for Company X and I would like to use the next 20 minutes to talk to you about our current research strategy. We have developed some interesting compounds which should be of major interest to this audience…*" then proceed to your second slide.

Or you could try something less formal like "*Thank you for those kind words. I am John Doe from Company X and I have been asked to talk about our strategy for whatever. I will talk for around 20 minutes then I will be more than happy to answer any questions you may have*".

And finally...

The end of your speech is just as important as the beginning. You do not want to fizzle out, but instead you want to go out with a bang! Make the ending memorable – use a quote, or a statistic, or something interesting.

If you are using slides when you give your speech, have a black blank slide as your final slide so you can show this, then end with a graceful "*Thank you for your attention*" (say this, don't put it on a slide) or whatever you feel most comfortable saying. As you rehearse, try to keep in your mind the opening and ending of your speech so that you can perfect these.

Channel the Adrenaline

Use the force

"I wish I was somewhere else", *"Oh God, why me..."*, *"I wish I didn't have to do this..."*. These negative thoughts are fairly common shortly before it is our turn to speak. The adrenaline is pumping, and the person before you is speaking, or the Chairman is introducing you.

The problem is, you are not really listening to what they are saying since you are so involved in your own small world of fear and anxiety. You need to take control of the adrenaline, and not let it control you.

Used well, anxiety can give you a real edge and make you appear confident even when you feel quite the opposite.

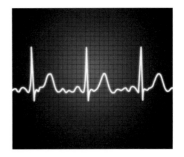

As we have seen, adrenaline is designed to help you succeed in battle or run away. It heightens the senses. If you can control your emotions, smile as you walk towards the lectern and appear calm, you will have taken the first step towards control.

Get through the first couple of slides, using the sentences you have written and practiced and you will feel much better. You can then start to improvise with the material, and avoid sounding scripted. Once you start, and you have found your voice, the flow will continue and you will convince yourself and the audience that you are in control, and that you are enjoying presenting this information to them. The emphasis again is on the *strong beginning*, keeping any tremor disguised (don't start using a laser pointer right at the beginning or your hand may be shaking visibly – later on in the speech the tremor will largely be gone). The audience will not sense your anxiety and certainly after two or three slides few would imagine you were anxious at all.

We have already discussed visualization of success when speaking. As you go through the talk keep reminding yourself that the whole event is going well, and the audience is enjoying listening to you. Look round the room to reassure yourself that they are attentive and appearing to be listening to what you are saying.

Practice!

Practice is boring

Practice is repetitive but it does bring its own rewards. Like a musician practicing scales it is something we have to do if we want to achieve that perfect public speaking experience. Many people don't practice much but they are the ones who forget what comes next, the ones who overrun their time slot because they have misjudged the time it takes to give the speech, and the ones who look less polished. Those who truly practice reap the benefits.

Practice begins on day one

As you craft the speech you should be saying the sentences out loud. Do they make sense? Are the words clumsy? Change them if this is the case. Do the graphics fit the words you will use? If they look good, keep them. If they do not, then change them.

If you are giving a talk using no visuals, break the speech into its component parts: beginning, middle and end. Work on each section separately and jot down subheadings which will match the major points you will be developing as you talk.

Index cards are very useful since you can sit quietly, with no distractions and design your speech. Put one heading on each card. If you are talking for 20 minutes, aim to use about 20 cards. Put down a few words under the heading on each card – these words will be used when you deliver the speech (although you will not read directly from cards when you give the speech).

Hot tip

Practicing is boring, but remember – the whole purpose is to engrain your topic into your head so you appear slick when you finally give the speech. Don't cut corners and try to "wing it". Put the effort in and get it right.

...cont'd

Talk yourself through the entire speech, moving from card to card to see if it makes sense and to ensure the flow is logical.

If it is, and no more needs to be added, staple the cards together to "fix" the speech. If you still need to work on some aspects then leave the cards loose but number them sequentially.

Once the speech is the way you want it, use a timer or stop watch and go through the talk – speaking more slowly than usual – and see if you can fit the talk into the time you have been allotted.

If you cannot, work out why this is. Too much material? Remove the less useful information. Are you spending too much time on one aspect? Try to slim this down or omit it completely.

Carry the cards with you in your bag or briefcase and practice on the bus, subway, over lunch.

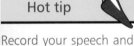

Hot tip

Record your speech and put it on your iPod, or write it on some cards and carry these with you so you can practice anywhere.

Put it on a CD or MP3 player and play it back to yourself in the car! Or read through your talk while you are in the parking lot waiting for your colleague to arrive!

By practicing extensively you will embed the main points in your head and you will remember the flow when it comes time to give the real talk.

Rather than carry the entire card set onto the stage, keep one card containing the titles of the cards written down in order. Keep this card in your jacket pocket and bring it out when you stand up to speak. You can use it as an aid, to make sure you are sticking to the script, but because you have practiced so much you will not need a script since you will recall the contents of the cards simply by glancing at the titles on the single card you have with you.

I'm Enjoying Myself

Smile, compose yourself and look like you are enjoying the occasion even if you're not! This is easier said than done but with time, practice and patience you will eventually not fear giving speeches. Or at least you will get the fear level down to an acceptable point where it does not interfere with your day-to-day activities, and the anticipation of giving a talk will not dominate your thoughts (this will happen in the early days).

Once you get past the first few slides, and your opening sentences have been delivered (uneventfully), you will start to relax. In fact, you will be unable to maintain the high level of anxiety you had at the beginning of the speech. You will feel the adrenaline levels drop, and your heart rate will slow down. Still nothing untoward has happened and you can start to "enjoy" the experience. Look round at the audience. Do they look interested? Are they nodding in agreement as you speak? This positive reinforcement should bolster your confidence and give you a real boost.

Don't forget

As you get used to giving speeches you will start to enjoy it. You may not believe this now, but it really is true!

People who give talks regularly, or act on stage, or play music to a public audience, find that they soon settle down after the initial few moments have passed. The occasion then takes over and the performance, boosted by a little adrenaline, takes over.

Eventually, especially if you follow the advice here, your public speaking ventures will reach this level and you will become more confident as time goes on. You will find you are no longer rooted to the spot (nerves) but instead you will start moving round the stage, varying your pace to maintain the audience interest even more, and ultimately you will become a real pro and have many tricks at your fingertips to raise the level of your performance way above the average seen in most organizations.

Summary

- Most people fear public speaking. In fact, most people dread public speaking and would probably do anything to avoid having to stand up in public and deliver a speech

- Nagging doubts about performance, and the feeling we need to be perfect, make us so anxious we often underperform

- Learning to cancel out negative thoughts, dwelling instead on the positives, helps immensely in delivering a great speech

- Anxiety is complex. Much of it reflects an underlying lack of confidence in our ability to project ourselves, perform under pressure, handle the technologies involved, and answer questions with authority

- The audience is there for you. They have come to hear what you have to say, and they want you to succeed. We often see them as the enemy which only adds to our anxiety state

- Dry mouth, shaking and loss of concentration are common when giving a speech. These are all symptoms of a heightened adrenaline response

- This can cause many presenters to fall apart but in many ways, the adrenaline can be used to your advantage – giving you an edge which you would not have at other times

- Sometimes medical treatment, in the form of drugs, can help reduce anxiety levels but in general psychological approaches are superior

- Using alcohol as a crutch is never advisable, partly because your performance will be impaired rather than enhanced, and there is a risk of addiction if you use alcohol frequently

- One sure way of allaying anxiety is to be well prepared, both mentally and physically. If you really know your topic, and have practiced sufficiently, your anxiety levels will be far lower

- Practice your speech wherever and whenever you can

- Eventually, you will get to the stage where you may be slightly keyed up before a speech but you will dread the event less and even start to enjoy the occasion!

3 Planning Your Speech

Giving a clear message is critical for a good speech. You need to define your key messages, do your research collating information, then organize this into a coherent structure. After this, you can start to draft your speech.

It's Not About You!

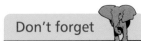

Don't forget

It's not about you. You need to first consider the audience and what they want to hear.

It really isn't, though you may be obsessed about your appearance, your delivery, your content, your handling of the Q&A session and so you overlook the fact that the whole reason for organizing the speech in the first place is to satisfy an audience. The people attending to listen to you have specific needs. They may have traveled a long way to hear you and they will have definite expectations. Or if you are the Best Man at a wedding the guests will have some expectations too.

You will never write or deliver a good speech if you concentrate solely on yourself. You must consider the listeners' needs before you put your speech together. That way, you will get the balance right and the audience is likely to be satisfied with the outcome.

On the other hand, if you write the speech you think they *should* hear you may be disappointed with the outcome and the feedback you get.

Focus on the audience

- Be passionate and enthusiastic about the speech. This is infectious and will get them enthused

- Consider their needs when drafting your speech – find out exactly what they want you to talk about

- Keep the content relevant to the audience. Don't just show off all you know about the subject. If it's not relevant to them, it's a waste of time and energy

- Make sure the content is up to date and fresh. They will not thank you for showing old data

- Try to show them how the content relates to them, rather than just present abstract ideas. This will allow them to see how the information can be used for them personally

- Try to make the speech informative without being too data heavy. Try to entertain as you speak

- Create a story and take them through from beginning to end. This will make it less of a chore for them to listen

- Use whatever props, visuals, or slides as long as they complement what you say. You and your words should be the main focus

Who Are You Speaking To?

The first thing you must check, after someone has invited you to talk, is the make-up of the audience. You may be speaking to real experts in the field or they may have little knowledge of the topic. If you get this the wrong way round it will be disastrous. If you lecture in very simple terms to people who know a great deal about the subject they will be insulted; if, on the other hand you deliver a highly complex speech to people who know little you will lose them after the title slide.

The organizers should be able to tell you how many people are expected to be there and who they are. If they are not sure how much they know ask them to find out and get back to you.

If you are attending a family occasion such as a wedding or birthday, you will know who is attending. The contents of these speeches will be family-oriented so becoming too technical will not arise. But it is still worth checking about the nature of a family gathering since people of different religions attend weddings and if you start telling jokes based on religion you could be in for a stormy time. Cultural, sexual and religious beliefs must be handled sensitively and, as a rule of thumb, these topics are best avoided completely.

All audiences are not the same!

Some people will put together a set of slides or a speech, and use the same ones for every event which deals with roughly the same topic. Such speakers may be busy and feel they have little time to put together new presentations. Although this does, indeed, save you time, the problem with this approach is that the material you present is the same irrespective of whether you are speaking to top experts or a group of school children.

Polished presenters would never fall into this trap. They seek high evaluation scores so they will do their utmost to ensure that the material they present is "personal" to the audience in question.

Hot tip

Tailor your speech for the specific audience you are speaking to. Try to avoid using a "one size fits all" approach.

What Do They Expect to Learn?

For academic or business meetings there is always an agenda. You have been asked for one of a number of different reasons. You may be expected to *educate* the audience about new technologies or procedures. They will generally have a fair degree of understanding of the subject area and you will be adding to that knowledge with new information.

You may be expected to change or *influence behavior*. Perhaps there are new ways of working on a specific area of the company's business. The management may have decided to have a team away day where different members of the team are asked to present the new methods to the whole group. Presumably you are a senior member of the team and one who has grasped the impact of the new methods and so they have chosen you as the person to share the ideas with the others within the team.

Teaching and education

Here the audience will expect to be given a fairly didactic style lecture, with learning points stated at the beginning. There is little scope for much improvisation or spontaneity.

Business speeches

There are many types of business meeting. Your audience may be colleagues within your department. Or you may be speaking to large groups of your colleagues within the company. What they expect to hear depends on the setting, but usually business meetings are intended to sell things, or inform colleagues of developments or provide updates on progress.

Social gatherings

These are usually fun events, on the whole, and learning is not really a major component of your speech. You are usually just there to entertain them.

The Goals of Your Speech

Before putting pen to paper or finger to keyboard, get a plain notepad and write down the main points of your talk. What three or four things would you most want your audience to remember a week after you have given your speech? Keep the list short, since if you think they should recall 10 items you are asking for trouble. Less is more, so three or four should be the maximum.

For example, looking at a new treatment for a disease the points which would feature in a conclusion would be:

- Current treatment is not satisfactory since it is not efficacious and is associated with toxicities

- There is a new treatment which has been developed

- The new treatment has been thoroughly tested in drug trials and is both effective and safe

- The new treatment should be used in place of the existing treatment

This is a simple list and is very easy to remember. The flow is logical and it is likely that an audience member would be able to recall this several weeks later.

The goals of your talk will depend on several of the factors we have discussed already, such as the audience's expectation and prior knowledge, your role (educator, informer or influencer of behavior), how long you have to talk, what emphasis they want you to stress, as well as the material being discussed by your co-speakers if there is a panel of presenters in a session.

Only once you have the goals written down should you start to plan the actual speech and undertake your research. If your goals are wrong then you will waste valuable time researching unnecessary topics.

Hot tip

Work out what the goals of your speech are – up-front, then the rest should fall into place.

Getting Started

Like most things in life we all need a nudge to get us started. If you are asked to give a talk in 12 months' time, I would be astonished if you were to start work on your talk now. Human nature being what it is we tend to leave things as late as possible. Is this because we are lazy? I don't think so. We are busy people, we have demanding careers and many other issues both at work and home to contend with and so a presentation in 12 months' time slips down the to-do list and ends up as a low priority issue, and probably quite rightly so.

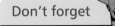

Don't forget

Start your planning as early as possible. This will give you lots of time to gather material, write your speech and hone it to perfection.

46

Also, we have already seen that adrenaline, if used well, can give us an edge. With a talk so far ahead it is very unlikely there will be any adrenaline flowing and so there will be no sense of urgency.

However, as the talk looms closer the adrenaline will start to kick in and we will feel more stressed about the presentation, and start to think about it more and more until we reach a point where we really must make a start if only to allay our conscience.

Usually four weeks ahead of a speech is enough time to start putting the whole thing together, although before this it is a good idea to clarify the remit of your task with the organizers of the meeting to ensure you really do know what's expected of you.

So, one month ahead of the speech, get your goals sorted out, and try to get the headings for some of your sections or slides on index cards or a notebook. Carry the cards or notebook with you and when you get a moment flick through the titles and see what ideas come into your head. Many will be irrelevant but do not worry about that right now – just get your thoughts down on paper. You can cross off the less useful ones later when it comes time to refine your thoughts.

Let your thoughts and the ideas in the book mature for a week or two before you start being ruthless and throwing out the irrelevant information or ideas.

Get Your Thoughts Together

Brainstorming, or some form of free flowing thought, is great for writing speeches. We already have our notebook or index cards with many ideas jotted down. Place these in front of you alongside the key messages you want to get across (this helps you focus on relevant ideas) then see what else you can add.

Once you have lots of ideas go through these and see if any are obviously of no use in this speech and remove them. Leave yourself only the ideas which are relevant to this presentation and this audience. Do these ideas support your conclusion, and most importantly, do they reinforce your key messages?

If they do, that's great. If not, have a break then come back and go through the whole stack and see what you need to add to reinforce your message.

Try using an outliner program or mind-mapping software to help you organize the specific order of the sections of your speech. This book, for example, was planned using Microsoft Word's outliner option, but any outliner will do. An outliner lets you assign text to various levels from 1–7 where 1 is a top level title and 2–7 are subheadings, sub-subheadings and so on. If you don't like the placement of a title and its text you can drag it to a more suitable part of the speech.

Mind-mapping software lets you make associations between headings and text. These can be dragged around in order to improve the flow. You cannot write a speech using mind-mapping but you can crystallize your thoughts which will result in a superior speech when you come to write it. There are many mind-mapping programs available for all computing platforms. Some are free or shareware, while others are much more expensive. In the end it comes down to esthetics – some programs are more polished but they all allow you to develop your thoughts, relationships between different items and the best bit of all is the way mind-mapping helps you work out new threads and relationships between items that you might not have thought of otherwise. It's worth downloading a mind-mapping program trial to see if it suits your way of working.

By now you will have lots of ideas and threads on paper or in a program and you need to get these assembled into a near finished talk.

Hot tip

If you find your thoughts are too disorganized try an outliner or a mind mapping program.

Define Your Key Message

We have already discussed the need for strong key messages but it is worth repeating here. Generally when we hear a talk we remember little detail of the speech. We may remember some of the graphics if they are particularly good or bad, and we can generally remember whether a speaker was good or bad. But the actual detail of the speech is usually vague. Because of this, a critical part of your speech is the final part, where you bring together the points you have been discussing and formulate a conclusion to the speech.

Some speakers have too many bullet points in their conclusion slides and end up with "Conclusions 1", "Conclusions 2" and so on. It is best to avoid having too many "Conclusions" and instead, limit this to one slide with three or four bullets only. The audience will not be able to remember more than that.

So how do you make sure your "Conclusions" are supported by the speech you have just delivered?

You write the Conclusion first then write the speech around that. You need to decide what it is you want them to learn from your talk, write the ending then generate the content that builds up to that conclusion.

Here's a simple conclusion slide that helps students understand anemia. Bullets have been used in this slide but it would look fine if the bullets were omitted.

Summary

- Anaemia is common
- Has many causes
- May be inherited or acquired
- Investigate by assessing clinical picture & MCV
- Start with simple investigations

Get it Down on Paper

Computers are great tools for writing, graphics, manipulating data and many other boring tasks but they do not necessarily help creativity. Sitting in front of a blank page on a screen can be quite inhibiting. Plus there are so many other distractions that may prevent you being creative, such as your web browser and email program which may be receiving email the whole time.

From personal experience, I think the best way to plan any speech is to switch off the PC and sit somewhere quietly with a notepad and pencil. You can sketch down your ideas and draw lines between the various components to show how they interrelate.

- Jot down your key messages first, on a separate page

- Place this in front of you so you can see the key messages at all times. As you note down the points you want to discuss during your speech keep checking the key points to see if these fit with your key messages

- If you are giving an informal speech at a wedding or leaving party there is less need for key messages (although some form of conclusion is still useful, such as *"Well, Jim has been with the company now for 30 years, and during that time he has achieved X and transformed the way we do Y, and so we all wish him well in his retirement."*)

You could use a proforma for all your presentations, which will help you allocate the time required for preparation, learn about the audience, work out what you are going to say and using which particular aids. Proformas for many speaking events can be found in Chapter 10.

Do Your Research!

So you have accepted the challenge to talk to a group of people, and you have clarified the topic and the main purpose of your speech. Now you need to gather some information which you will use in your speech. What kind of resources are available to you? In this new media age we have the Internet to help us. This is a fantastic resource which is growing at a phenomenal rate. There seems to be little that cannot be found on the Internet. Most people use the web as a source of factual material, images, videos and other material. The problem you face when using the Internet is information overload! You need to sift through the information and select the material that is useful for your talk and resist the temptation to cram your speech full of detail just because it's there. Organizing the material you find is a major challenge which we will discuss later in this chapter.

Don't forget

Do your research. You want your information to be complete and up to date.

Books such as autobiographies and textbooks are still used quite heavily in the sciences and health-related fields. The graphics in books are generally of good quality and can be scanned to use in slides (although beware of copyright restrictions). If you have sufficient time before you give your speech it is worth reading through an authoritative book on your chosen topic to see what ideas emerge which you can use in your speech. There may be aspects of the subject you had not considered, so jot down snippets in your pad. You can use these later when it comes time to draft your speech.

Letters and other documents can be useful especially if you are discussing historical aspects of a subject. If you or a colleague has any old letters which might add color to your talk, you could scan these and drop them into a slide to make your talk more interesting (rather than just read sections of the letter out to the audience).

Museums and art galleries are full of material that can be used for speeches since these are very visual environments. Obviously these are only of any value if your speech covers arts, sciences or related topics. For business speeches these resources are less useful.

Talking to colleagues is useful, especially after you have drafted out a rough plan of your speech. They will likely know the field fairly well (if the speech is linked to your work) and may be able to suggest items that you had overlooked. They may also have documents, images or text related to the subject. They may even have a previous speech on the topic. You could use some of this in your own speech. If you are going to speak at a family or social gathering you could run through an outline of your speech with your partner, parents or sibling to make sure nothing is omitted and also to check you have not included anything which might offend anyone.

Plan ahead

- Decide what you need for your speech

- Do this early to avoid rushing around at the last minute looking for material

- You might simply want some key facts and figures – ask someone within the company for these

- You may need graphs or other visuals. Obtain the data and plot the graphs and charts or borrow from a colleague who may have already presented these figures and have them in spreadsheet form or as a graph

- You may need some artwork, photographs, or line art. High quality artwork can be bought through Shutterstock and other web-based companies (see Chapter 11)

Take Clippings From the Web

Whenever we do a Web-based search for information we end up going down blind alleys, and visit sites that are very diverse. Sometimes they contain lots of useful information and sometimes they contain just one picture that might be useful later. How can you organize this material so that it can be used later?

Avoid printing – save the trees!
You could print off every page from the sites you visit but this is wasteful and you will end up with a stack of paper which you will then have to sift through to find the useful material all over again.

Screenshots
You could feasibly take screenshots of all the pages and store these electronically but again, you will need to go through all of these at a later stage in order to find the scraps of information that may be useful.

Clippings
There are software programs that help you capture Web-based information which you can store for later use. Many of these software programs allow you to search *within* the material. Some will even let you search for text within images which is a major advantage (generally text which is part of a graphic cannot be searched).

Evernote
This is one program that appears very useful in this respect. It is available from *http://evernote.com*. There are versions for Windows, Mac, iPhone and other cell phones. After creating an Evernote account you can start collecting Web clippings. These are stored in folders that you create.

The beauty of this type of system is that the clippings are stored on a remote server and your local drive so you can access the information wherever you are, and using any computer. Each time you launch Evernote it syncs your local data with the server so that they contain the same information.

There are too many Web clipping services to list here but you might want to take a look at yodlee2go (at *http://www.tucows. com*), Microsoft OneNote (*http://www.microsoft.com*), clipmarks (clipmarks.com) and Google Notebook (*http://www.google.com/ notebook*).

Screenshot of the Evernote homepage:

Evernote in action, showing folders for projects, each containing Web pages, PDFs and other related documents.

It's No Joke!

Beware

Using humor in a speech is a high risk strategy (unless you are at a social gathering, and even in this setting you need to be careful).

Can you use humor when you give a speech? Most of us have sat through speeches where the speaker has told a joke which has bombed. It is very difficult to recover from this, especially if the joke is sexist or religious. For this reason it is much safer to steer clear of telling jokes during your speech unless you are giving a Best Man's speech at a wedding, where you might be telling jokes involving the groom. You would be forgiven for using this type of humor in this setting. But in general, jokes do not work very well during lectures or speeches especially if you are lecturing in another country since things which are funny in one culture may not be seen as humorous in another.

Humor is quite different to telling jokes. Something which is humorous may make us smile or nod in agreement and many speakers use humor to lighten up their speeches.

The best type of humor is probably self-deprecating humor, where you relate a funny personal anecdote about yourself. Audiences warm to this, because it makes you human and gets you on their level. They will relate to you better and will probably pay more attention to the rest of your speech. "*Personally speaking I always thought that … but hey, what do I know?*" This is more humorous if you are a major expert in the subject being discussed especially if the audience knows this.

The use of humor does not come naturally to all of us, and when we are nervous it can be difficult to inject humor into our speeches. One of our major fears when giving a speech is the humor that fails – the humor where no-one smiles or even notices that you were being humorous. "*Why did I say that? I won't do that again*". It can be off-putting. So the rule of thumb is, if you feel confident, try some humor but if you are nervous and not so confident, stick to the main speech and build on your experiences.

Liven Up the Speech

Real life stories can liven up a speech

This follows on from the use of humor in speeches. If you can make your speech personal, people will warm to you and listen more intently.

Try to bring in experiences from your own practice. If you have a method of working that seems to deliver results then tell them about it. You could say something like "*Ten years ago my company was failing to bring in new customers. I decided that we should use a new approach and I introduced X. As a consequence, our business increased by 50% a year and our share value has rise to $100*". The audience can relate both to you, and to the story you have told them. It has ceased to be something abstract and has now become something real which has much more meaning to them in their work.

Make an impact!

How can you break the mold when you get up to speak? How can you really get the audience's attention and stand out from the crowd? Start your presentation with a bang such as "*Did you know that a rat can last longer without water than a camel?*" Or "*100 million trees are cut each year to generate junk mail*". This type of statement wakens the audience up. Speakers seldom use openers like this, and so this is like a breath of fresh air to the audience. You can, of course, sprinkle these types of facts throughout your presentation but the most dramatic way is to use it right at the beginning.

Quotations are great for getting the audience to listen. You can use books of quotes or go online to:

http://www.quotationspage.com/

http://www.quoteland.com/

http://quotations.about.com/

http://www.woopidoo.com/business_quotes/

Slides as Audiovisual Aids

With the invention of Aldus Persuasion some years ago speakers had the ability to generate their own slides which could be projected onto a screen. PowerPoint soon followed, and the entire worlds of business, science, medicine, the arts, and other professions started to add slide presentations to speeches.

Slides are very useful supports for your speeches since they can contain facts, figures and visuals that can be shown as you deliver your speech. When used properly, a good set of slides complement the speech beautifully and make the event more memorable for the audience. A bonus feature of these slide programs is that handouts can be printed and given to the audience so they can re-read the content at a later date.

Unfortunately, most of us use our slides as a repository for all the information we intend to cover in our speech. Rather than commit to memory we now rely on our slide deck since we can put lots of useful (and useless) information onto the slides and use these as prompts as we go through our speech.

The problem is this makes most speeches and presentations today fairly boring. Because the slides contain so much information we can stop listening to the speaker and just read the slides. Or we can have a nap and read the handout.

But the slides should not contain your entire speech. They should only contain a limited amount of text, which should be there to reinforce what you say. The slides should (ideally) be text-light and should be visual, containing graphics and images that complement the speech which you will deliver orally (not on the screen).

We do not have space here to delve into slide design but the following pointers may help you create useful slides:

- Try to use only a few slides

- Keep the design simple with a plain background and use only one or two different font families

- Try to avoid using bullets on the slide, but place your greatest emphasis on the graphic elements (i.e. pictures) with a few words on each slide

This makes your slides more visually attractive and also means the audience will spend more time listening to you since there will be little to read on the slides.

Beware

Slides are great, in small doses. There is a tendency for slide shows to dominate and become the main feature.

The slide below is crammed with far too much text. The audience will read this and will not listen to you.

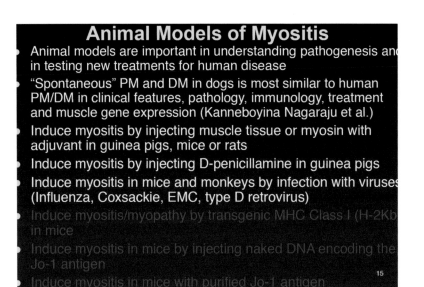

The second slide is easier on the eye and gives lots of scope for discussion.

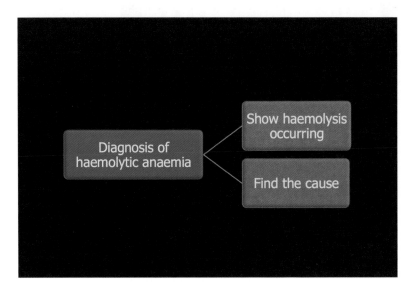

Information Overload

You will probably know a great deal about your subject and you will be trying to impress but don't try to show the audience how much you know. Be selective in what you say and show them.

People who are not used to speaking in public or giving presentations generally include too much information and use too many slides. There is no absolute rule about how many slides you should use if you are using PowerPoint, but we are generally taught that one slide for every minute allocated to your speech should work. This is fine if you are using old-fashioned slides with about six bullet points per slide. But if you decide to only use one word per slide you could have 50 or even 100 slides for your 20 minute session.

It is better to use less time for a presentation than overrun your time. The audience will never object to a talk that ends after 15 minutes instead of 20, but they will not be pleased if a 20 minute speech becomes a 25 or 30 minute ordeal.

If you are organized and have broken your speech down into chunks you should be able to provide sufficient background information to allow them to understand the main points of your presentation.

Hot tip

Keep your audiovisuals, like slides, to a minimum and try to keep them lean and free of clutter.

- Keep the word count down and the graphics content high

- Break the content down into major sections first – Introduction, Main Body and Conclusions

Get Organized!

Use an outliner

These have been around for years and there are many to choose from – some free and some for purchase. If you own Microsoft Word you can use the outliner option within Word to write your speech.

Basically, it uses different styles or "levels". Level 1 is major heading, Level 2 is a subheading, Level 3 is the text that goes with the Level 2 heading, and Level 4 is a further subheading.

The beauty of an outliner is that you can plan your speech as a series of headings then later fill in the detail. The fact that you can hide the detail helps focus your thoughts.

If you find that some sections do not fit well and you would prefer to move them to another chapter, just collapse the outline down to, say, Level 1 (so you only see the big titles), then drag to wherever you think it fits better. All the text corresponding to that header will be moved too. Of course, you could just cut and paste text in a word processor but outliners make it so much easier.

Here are some screenshots of the Word outliner which was used to write this book:

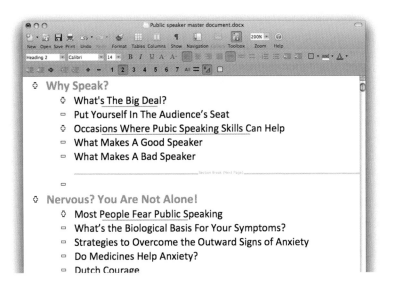

Only Levels 1 and 2 are shown here. The main text was created in the Level 3 and 4 styles.

Summary

- When giving a speech, remember it is not about you. Understandably your main concerns will be about your performance, your appearance, your content but the event has been arranged for the audience so try to focus on them when you write your speech

- Do your homework and find out who the audience is. They will have specific expectations and you will need to create your content with this in mind

- Ask whoever invited you to speak what your role is. Are you there to inform, entertain, advise, instruct, persuade, or sell?

- Start writing with your specific goals in mind. Make sure you are very clear about what these are. Keep the goals near you so you can refer to them as you write. This helps you construct your speech and, more importantly, helps keep you on track

- Initially, it is best to jot down ideas on paper. Resist the temptation to start typing into the computer. Keep your head clear from distractions, and this means email, web browsing and other PC-related activities. In fact, it is best not to be anywhere near the computer when you first start to create your content – keep distractions to a minimum

- Research the subject well, using books, journals, the Internet, and any other resource. Make sure your content is fresh

- Avoid trying to use jokes or too much humour, but you can liven up your speech with quotes or other notable information

- Slides are great for presenting data and to provide a framework for your talk. But avoid trying to make them the star of the show. They won't be, and neither will you

- Limit the amount of information you show to the audience. Too much and you will lose them

- Try to keep your thoughts and ideas organized. It is too easy to lose control and find yourself surrounded by bits of paper or clippings from the Web. Use specific notepad and Web clipping software to store your resources. This helps you organize them and find them later

4 Practice Makes Perfect

You cannot practice a speech too much. You need to decide which words to use, and which graphics fit the presentation. Timing is crucial and you need to rehearse out loud in order that your speech will fit into the time slot you have been given.

Benefits of Practicing

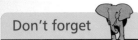

Don't forget

Practice, practice and practice some more. This will help ensure your speech is polished and slick.

As children we are told that *"Practice makes perfect"* and this is no truer than when we are giving a speech. Few of us are able to deliver an off-the-cuff speech that flows correctly, using all the right words and concludes elegantly. It just doesn't happen. You may have written a great speech but at some point you are going to have to face an audience of colleagues, peers or family and deliver your speech. This does not mean reading it aloud to them but instead you will use cues such as slides or headings on a card to lead you through the presentation in a step-wise logical progression.

Practicing a speech is one of the most important aspects to developing a great presentation. Unfortunately it is one aspect which is often overlooked, especially when we are short of time. As we plan the speech we tend to minimize the time taken to explain things, and when it comes time to actually deliver the speech we find that we run out of time because diagrams that looked straightforward are actually quite complex and take much longer to explain than you thought.

Practicing your speech is therefore important in order to determine

- The content of the speech

- The content of the slides

- The timing of the whole speech, making sure it can be fitted in to the time allowed

- To ensure your conclusion fits with all the speech leading up to the conclusion

So, as you plan your diary after you agree to speak, make sure you factor in sufficient practice time.

Edit the Speech

How to practice and edit your speech

The best way to practice would probably be to use the venue where you will be speaking with the screen and laptop and other facilities but few of us have this luxury.

Once your slides have been designed, or you have written the headings for your speech if you are not using slides, go through the entire speech from beginning to end gauging the material (but not editing at this stage). How does it sound? Does each slide or heading flow logically? Go right to the end and run through the conclusion slide. Do the points on the conclusion fit with the tone and messages of the overall speech? Maybe not.

Then go through again from the beginning looking at the text on the slides. Are all the titles and body text consistent in size throughout the presentation? Has there been any font substitution – make sure the same fonts have been used throughout.

Elements of the slides such as headers, body text and footers all have a position on the slide. If the headers change position from slide to slide it spoils the look of the slides. If need be, check what position the headers or text should be and manually adjust any that are wrong.

Are the graphics appropriate? Cropped as necessary and placed in the correct area of the slide?

Use the Slide Sorter view in PowerPoint (or whichever program you are using) and look at the overall balance of text and images. Does your whole presentation look consistent? If not, adjust it so that it does.

Once you have sorted out the content of the slides or index cards, or whatever you are using as an aid, you need to start practicing saying the words out loud. Most people like to practice alone. Run through the slides on the screen or print off a copy of the material and try to imagine you are actually delivering your speech and use the words you plan to use on the day.

Are you expressing yourself clearly? Are you stumbling over any sections? If you are, then spend time on these areas to make sure you get rid of any rough edges. And don't forget to *slow down* your speech – this will help you pronounce difficult words and will also make sure your speech fits into the time allocated.

Get Them Excited

Sprinkle your speech with exciting words

Some topics can be boring, but even exciting topics can be made boring if delivered by the wrong presenter. Using exciting words throughout your speech can get the audience excited and keep them there. You want to be *motivational* if possible. You would like them to remember your presentation for the right reasons, and not because you were dull!

Examples of exciting words are: *absolutely, authentic, crammed, dynamic, direct, improved, powerful, astonishing, professional, personalized, practical, secure, unparalleled, unsurpassed, discerning, empowered, innovative.*

Where to start?

- Keep smiling

- The excitement starts the minute you get out of your seat. You should be walking very confidently towards the podium and smiling. Make sure you catch the eyes of all sections of the audience – left, center and right

- Make sure they know you are really pleased to be there

- You have some really interesting information to share with them

- If you are truly passionate about your subject you will not need a book to teach you how to convey this to the audience. Sometimes, however, even though we are really excited about a project or business when speaking one to one, we appear slightly robotic in front of a large group. This is essentially a confidence issue. Speakers who are nervous and underconfident seem to dry up and lack any real sparkle when they are stressed. If this sounds like you, try to spend some time working on anxiety reduction. This will help you relax into the talk and the "real" you will take over!

- You can get the audience whipped up into a frenzy if you make it absolutely clear why your speech is so important – what's in it for them? Lots! They will understand the subject better, their sales will improve, they will work better as a team, they will have a greater idea of the company's vision for the future, they will see where the Research & Development is leading

Speak More Slowly

Teach yourself to speak more slowly

Some people speak slowly naturally. Others speak quickly and when stressed, will talk even more quickly. This makes it difficult to follow the speech especially if English is not your first language.

Does it matter? Maybe you feel you are still fairly eloquent even when you speak quickly, but the fact is that people need to hear things in bite sized chunks. This is especially true of presentations. You need to feed them a little bit, wait for it to sink in, then move on to the next slide or topic.

If you are speaking on a subject which is not wholly familiar to the audience, they will be listening carefully, assimilating what you are saying. They need natural pauses to do this.

If you speak very quickly, moving from slide to slide like an express train, the audience will be thinking about slide 4 while you are on slide 14. Eventually they will stop being able to take in new information and the rest of your speech will fail.

Adrenaline makes us talk very fast almost to the point of babbling if we are very stressed out! Hopefully this will be less marked as you go through your presentation and will be most pronounced at the beginning when stress levels are high.

- At the start of your speech, try very consciously to slow down

- For a native English-speaking audience you need to speak *much more slowly* than you normally would

- For a *non* English-speaking audience you need to speak even slower. This means you cannot use the same amount of information in your talk for both audiences. It is unfair to people for whom English is not their language to expect them to follow a presentation in a foreign language, with all the nuances and jargon you might use

- So keep it *simple* and keep it *slow*

- With lots of pauses between sentences and the slides

- Get a piece of paper or an index card and write "*Speak Slowly!*" in big letters and have this in front of you as you speak!

We speak more quickly when nervous. You will probably have to consciously slow your speech down to avoid racing through it.

Rehearse Out Loud

Rehearsal is a bore. It really is. There are so many other things to do it seems crazy to spend long hours rehearsing. Is it *really* necessary to practice that much? Yes, absolutely. If you want to appear polished, slick, and with perfect timing, yes it is really necessary.

Silent rehearsal

As you draft your speech and create your slides, if you are using these, run through the order of the headings by reading these through. You will spot any glaring errors, omissions, items placed in the wrong place quite quickly.

Tidy up the slide deck or speech and get it into the basic shape you feel would be best for the speech.

Rehearsing out loud

You may feel silly, but try to rehearse out loud, in your office, in the car, in the shower, on the mountainside – anywhere that you feel comfortable. Saying a word in your head and actually speaking it out loud is quite different. It only takes a fraction of the time to read to yourself and you can gauge how long a speech will take much more accurately if you say it out loud.

Sometimes there are words and phrases that look pretty straightforward when you read them. These are words that shouldn't cause problems but when you are nervous and speaking quickly (as you are when you give your talk) you may find you start to stumble over the words and have to correct yourself. If you are a veteran presenter this might not faze you. If you are a novice you will feel deeply embarrassed.

You can avoid all of this by *saying the words out loud*. You can hear how they sound. If it sounds good – that's great. If they sound odd, confused, awkward – you can change them now.

Record the speech

You could also try recording yourself giving your speech. How does it sound? Awkward? Natural? Listening to yourself should help you work out which bits are going to cause you problems.

Recording is also a great way of memorizing your speech without really memorizing it. You would never want to give your speech as a verbatim presentation but recording it and listening to it embeds the order of topics, making the presentation smoother.

Hot tip

Rehearsing out loud gives you a much better idea of how long your speech will last when you give it for real.

Timing is Everything

You will usually know how long you are meant to be speaking for. Try to deliver your speech in slightly less time. This gives you more time at the end for questions, and also makes the audience happy. They never object to a talk that ends early.

You could use the timer option in the presentation software, or if you are not using slides you could just stand up in your office and use a standard oven timer or stop-watch.

The picture below shows Apple Keynote's Presenter View. The slide on the left is the one that is shown to the audience. The slide on the right is the next slide in the sequence (the audience cannot see this one). There are two clocks: that on the left shows the time of day and on the right it shows how long you have been speaking.

Sadly, unless you are presenting from your own laptop this feature will not be available to you.

My presentation

First slide

Item One
Text

Item Two
Text

14:45:52

00:00:00

As you practice, if you find you are overrunning your time, you could trim some of the slides. You could take out some diagrams if they are very complex and likely to take some time to explain during your presentation. If you are overrunning seriously then you may have to remove some slides completely. It is better to have a presentation that is too short than too long.

Rehearse to Friends

Hot tip

If you don't want to
rehearse alone, why not
ask a friend or colleague
to act as the audience
and critique your
performance?

Would your friends or colleagues be willing to act as volunteers
to listen to your speech and critique your performance? Many of
us avoid using this method of rehearsal but in some ways, asking
family members to help identify areas of ambiguity is helpful.
They will probably not be experts in the area and so if you say
something confusing they are likely to pick this up.

At major medical conferences, oral presentations are very
prestigious. If your work has been accepted for an oral
presentation you are doing well. These talks are seen as being
like the storefronts of your departments or labs, and the senior
staff are always very anxious if an inexperienced presenter is
chosen to give the talk. For that reason, they insist on having
practice presentations for weeks before the actual event. During
these presentations many of the lab staff sit in, including the
senior guys. The person who will give the talk at the conference
will go through his or her presentation and will receive hints
and suggestions from the audience. After this, the presenter will
amend the slides and will present again on another day and again
receive criticism until the whole presentation is good enough.

This may seem quite arduous and somewhat scary but it is

better to make the major mistakes in front of your friends
and colleagues than have the whole thing happen in front of a
conference audience of hundreds or possibly thousands of people.

Rehearse at the Venue Too

What's to stop you practicing at the actual venue? Nothing, providing you get there early enough.

If you are using slides, get these loaded onto the laptop and ask the AV guys to talk you through the various bits of equipment you will be using, such as microphone, laser pointer, slide changers, and others. They will generally be doing other things like checking audio levels so you can take to the stage before everyone arrives and go through your slides. You can get used to seeing them projected onto the screen to the right or left of you.

Can you see them well?

Go to the back of the room and look at your slides. Can you still read the text? It is all too easy to work on our PCs creating slides that look (on the PC) fantastic only to find later that the text is too small or the lines on the graph cannot be seen.

Do you know how to move backwards as well as forwards through the slides?

Can you point to words or images using the laser?

Is there a screen on the podium where you can see your slides?

Try mainly to use this so you are facing forward and engaging the audience and avoid turning your back for long periods to point things out on the slides projected behind you.

Running through things using the real equipment generally helps reduce anxiety levels since you know what you are doing and can imagine standing there speaking to the audience when they arrive.

Annotate Your Handouts

Handouts are great for rehearsing your speech and for giving the audience. They are also very useful for jotting down things that you might otherwise forget. You could also use the "Notes View" in PowerPoint but often that feature is not available at conferences so do not rely on this.

Don't forget

Handouts are great for the audience but they are also useful for your own notes. Annotate them in big letters and refer to them, if necessary, when you give your speech.

If there are facts or figures that you are worried you might forget to mention, note these down on the handout next to the relevant slide. Use only one handout and make all your notes on this one set. While you are traveling to the meeting and while you are sitting in the audience waiting to speak you can go through your notes again. This will help ensure you mention things that are important to the talk but which are not actually on the slides themselves.

Use PowerPoint Notes

Microsoft PowerPoint, Apple Keynote, OpenOffice Impress, and others have a Notes feature. This usually appears as a text box below each slide into which you can type notes. Keep these brief and use a large font. Once you have made all your notes, print off a hard copy of your Notes pages and have this with you when you give your speech. Make sure you keep the hard copy page in sync with the one being presented on the screen or you will get muddled and the notes will then hinder rather than help you.

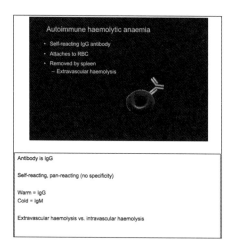

Quite often, simply the process of typing notes into the Notes Page in PowerPoint is enough to help you remember the complicated information.

Be Yourself

After all this practice, and the emphasis on achieving a polished performance, you might feel you have to speak in a different manner to your normal way of speaking.

In general it is best not to try to create a "speech" voice. Just think about how some people answer the phone using a very affected accent – it just sounds bad and pretentious. Your own voice will be fine but you will need to work on projecting your voice so that your speech is clear to all those in the audience, even if they are at the back of the room. We will discuss this further in Chapter 8.

Hot tip

Try to be as natural as possible when you speak.

Relax

It is difficult, I have to agree, to be completely comfortable facing a large audience, trying to appear enthused and passionate, while controlling equipment that you have never used and trying to sound authoritative. Some do it well, but they have usually done it many times before so they are not stressed by being up there performing.

How to appear confident

- Try to be as natural as is possible under the circumstances

- Speak in your normal voice but speak more deliberately, slowly and louder than usual

- Pause between slides, or if you are not using slides, simply pause where there is a natural break. Allow the audience to absorb the information

- You may not be relaxed when you first start to speak but after a few minutes you should start to relax

- Keep your focus on the audience and glance at your watch from time to time (place your wrist watch on the lectern or table so you can see it clearly)

- Remember to breathe naturally, too. Some people get carried away and say quite long sentences without breathing. This makes them sound breathless. Consciously tell yourself to take a breath!

- If you need to, stop, have a sip of water, then continue. This will build in a pause and will also give you time to catch your breath

Summary

- Professional presenters spend a huge amount of time practicing their speeches to make sure the words fit well, the content sounds right and the speech fits within the time allotted

- If you fail to rehearse you may stumble over words, forget what is in the speech and risk overrunning your time slot

- This is an insult to the audience since they will feel you have not taken the time to ensure your speech is polished

- As you go through your speech, keep editing the content

- If sections are redundant, remove them

- You can add new content as you go through but take care not to try to pack too much in since your time will be limited

- Think of ways to get the audience excited

- Use words and phrases that sound dynamic and energizing. This is especially true if you are trying to persuade or sell

- When anxious we tend to speak more quickly. Consciously slow down your speech

- Try to rehearse out loud, because if you "run through" a speech in your head, the timing will be very different to that when using the spoken word. When your deliver your speech for real you will be speaking, so practice using spoken words

- If you can, try rehearsing to friends and family. They will often pick up flaws in your arguments, or highlight areas which you have not explained well

- Try to get to the venue early and practice there, too

- Use your handouts for keeping notes. You may not need them but they are reassuring to have nearby

- Timing is important. Quite often you will be one of several speakers. If you overrun your time slot you will use up your question time or you may encroach on your colleagues' time

- If you finish early, don't worry. This gives you more time for questions and the audience will not complain

5 Props May Help

Some people can talk with no aids at all. Others are dependent on laptops, flip charts and other devices. Technology has advanced the art of speechmaking but it can also be your undoing if not used correctly.

The Naked Presenter

Some presenters need crutches like PowerPoint, microphones or flip charts to present. They feel naked just standing there talking. Keeping an audience interested just by chatting takes skill and confidence.

Of course, it depends on the subject and the situation. If you are talking to colleagues at work about progress on a project I am sure most of us could stand there and talk quite easily with no visuals or microphones. If you keep the content very focused, covering just a few major points, you will not require visuals or prompts. This type of speech is more like a conversation with a group of people.

However, it would not be a useful style for lecturing on academic or technically complex subjects although there are some great lecturers who can keep an audience transfixed just by standing there and talking. Often these are older scientists or physicians who have not fully adopted the PowerPoint way of doing things (an advantage, many would say) and who have always had to rely on analog devices like paper and pen, or blackboards as visuals.

How to tackle a naked presentation

- Be personable, friendly, assured

- Convey enthusiasm and passion as you would for any speech

- Devise a good story and take them through this

- Add color wherever possible – for example, tell stories about your own experiences

- Try to help them see how what you are saying fits in with their life or work

- Take questions throughout the presentation – this produces a to and fro effect where you speak then they speak, then it's back to you (like the successful TV programs "*An audience with ...*" where celebrities are quizzed by the audience)

- While you answer questions you can throw out more facts and anecdotes. Try to underline and reinforce the message you want to get across

- Keep them engaged by maintaining eye contact throughout and make sure they feel involved

Computer Presentation

In business, and many other professions, computer presentation has become the *de facto* standard. Irrespective of what needs to be presented, some PowerPoint slides are thrown together and the audience has to sit and listen (and read) a typical boring presentation.

Slides are not intrinsically bad, and slide presentations are not the problem. It is the people using the software who cause the problems because the slides are written like documents, full of bullet points, several levels of heading and few visuals.

If we could think more visually we would create slides that have a major visual impact, containing a great image or two and just a few words with few bullets.

The problem is we have been indoctrinated into using a standard style of slide because that's what people do, and we emulate the presentations we have sat through (though why we try to reproduce this when we find them so boring, remains a mystery).

If you do want to use a computer to present data or other information, try to think a little differently. Try not to use bullet points. If you must select a predefined template keep it very simple. Avoid having too many words and try to find some illustrations that tell the story, rather than add a garnish to your slide.

Video Presentations

Beware

Don't try to be flashy by adding video to your presentation. It adds another layer of complexity and there's more chance something will go wrong!

Years ago, showing a video during a meeting was a big thing. The speaker had to stop, the TV screen would be switched on and the video play button would be pressed. The audience would watch the video, after which the speaker would resume talking or showing 35mm slides, or a flip chart.

Now we can create *digital* videos. This means we can store them on hard drives and memory sticks and we can insert them into slide programs.

In theory, when the speaker reaches the slide containing the video clip, he or she will press the advance button and the digital video will play.

But it often goes wrong. If you are using a PC the slide will contain a link to the video but the video itself will not be embedded within the slide. This means you need to have the presentation file (e.g. .ppt) and the video file (in the correct format such as MPEG or WAV) in the same folder or the video will fail to play. On the Mac side the video is embedded in the .ppt file but the Mac only recognizes .mov and WMV. Other formats such as WAV and WMA will generate audio but no video.

To keep your life simple and stress free try to avoid using video.

If you must use video

If you absolutely must use it, ask the organizers what type of computer is being used at the venue. If it is a PC, ask which version of Windows it

is running. Make sure you get to the venue especially early and check that your video plays as expected. If not, fix it or remove it. Leave nothing to chance. Your reputation is at stake. If it works well – great. If not, your reputation may be damaged.

Using Prewritten Notes

You may be nervous and feel that a written speech might help you just in case you dry up while you are giving your speech. I have seen people use notes and sometimes they work. I have tried them myself but I find they get in the way. This is partly because you need to work out a system that keeps you on track. If you are on slide 40 you need to be able to identify the text that accompanies that slide. You then have to read this, and the flow of your presentation will be less natural.

One system of notes that is helpful is the use of the handout to note down hard to remember facts and figures. Sometimes when we are nervous our concentration is impaired and we forget some of the things we intend to say. If you print off a copy of your talk (handout) then note down, in big letters, the things you might forget, you can take this to the podium with you and have it in front of you so you can remember to mention the fact and also get the details correct.

Below is a set of prompts I have used for a medical conference involving about eight speakers and an audience of 100 attendees. I wanted to make sure I covered all the important points. I glanced at this from time to time but did not read it out loud.

Beware

Prewritten notes are fine for rehearsing but don't use for the speech itself. It makes you sound boring and stilted.

I am really pleased to see so many people here today for this Masterclass in Haematology.

First of all I need to thank the staff at the BMJ (**Christiane, Philippa, Natalie),** for putting all this together so smoothly and for not hassling the speakers too much in terms of getting slides in. You will all have copies of the speakers slides in your packs.

We have a **mixed audience** of haematologists, elderly care physicians, palliative care doctors, ITU and renal specialists and gastroenterologists.

We have tried to cover as much of the specialty as possible but haematology is a HUGE area and we cannot do it all in one day. We have tried to cover most of the exciting advances that have taken place over the last year or so.

Haematology was the first branch of medicine to exploit molecular biology techniques and we have seen how advances in molecular biology has helped explain the molecular pathology of disease – this in turn has led to major advances in drug development for blood disorders.

So we are covering:

Malignant and non-malignant disease

On the malignant side we are concentrating on:

      acute and chronic myeloid leukaemias

      as well as the **myeloproliferative disorders**

On the non-malignant side we will be discussing advances in red cell disorders as well as coagulation and platelets

To speakers: since the audience is fairly mixed we need to bear this in mind

Scripts and Prompts

I have seen scripted speeches used a few times. Each time was terrible. The speakers were nervous and rather than risk fluffing a few lines they preferred to read each word to us. Would I ever recommend this method for giving a speech? *No, never.*

One caveat, however, would be if someone had to deliver a press statement. These are scripted, contain the facts and are not intended to be interesting or entertaining. In this setting I think you can get away with reading from a script.

Where a script might come in useful, especially for the very nervous presenter, would be as something to read through several times before giving the speech – but without using the script for the real speech. The chances are if you have read through your script several times you are going to remember much of what it contains. If you have the added benefit of having a slide show to accompany your speech you are not going to go far wrong.

Prompt cards

These are definitely useful, especially for nervous speechmakers. Index cards can be used to draft your speech, as we have already seen. So why not use index cards containing a few words or phrases to jog your memory as you go through your presentation? Each time you hit the slide advance button, put the top card to the bottom of the pile and the card relevant to that slide will be visible. You may not need it (which is great), but if you do suddenly dry up you can glance down at the card and it will remind you of what you are meant to say to that slide.

Or even if you are just talking and not using any high tech equipment, cards are useful as prompts. Many TV presenters use these in chat shows to remind them of what they are supposed to be asking of their guests. No-one has a perfect memory and there is no shame in using prompts such as these so go ahead and use them if necessary.

Microphones

Most inexperienced presenters do not use microphones correctly, and end up emulating rock stars by having their lips pressed against the black foam, resulting in very poor sound quality. If you are talking to a small group of people you should not need a microphone. Learn to project your voice and speak with more volume than usual so that the people right at the back can hear you.

If you are talking to a very large group you will need to use a microphone. The AV technical staff will have set this up for you. Generally two types of microphone are used. The first is the fixed microphone. You stand at the lectern, face the audience and speak towards the microphone but at a distance of a foot or so from the microphone. If you turn your head away (to look at a slide) the volume will drop so try to keep facing the direction of the microphone as much as possible. Lapel microphones are popular. These are small clip-on devices that are wireless. They pick up your voice no matter which way you are facing, so this means you can roam around the room or stage and the volume level will remain constant.

Microphones are also very useful if the event is being recorded for audio, or video with audio. This is fairly common and it allows people who could not attend the event to hear what you said. The broadcast can be burned onto DVD or converted to a webcast.

Hot tip

Ask the AV technical staff how to use the microphone before the session starts.

Laser Pointers

Another much misused piece of equipment is the laser pointer. These have replaced wooden pointers since when we present at major meetings we may be 50 feet away from the projection screen, and even if we could get to the screen, these are too large for us to reach even if we had a stick.

Buy yourself a cheap laser pointer online or in a stationery store. The organizers will provide one but sometimes the batteries run out and the light is too feeble to be seen.

The pointer should be used to point out features on a complex graphic, or if you are using mainly text you should point to the occasional key word that you want them to see.

Try to avoid keeping it on for long periods, running along all lines of text, and definitely avoid pointing the laser at the audience since the light can be damaging to the eye.

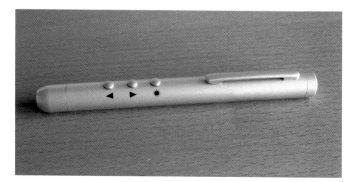

Beware

Laser pointers are dangerous if pointed directly at the eyes. Practice using one and only use it during your speech if you feel confident to do so.

Ideally when you want to point to a word or feature on a slide you should aim the laser at the foot of the slide then draw a line up to the word you wish to highlight, then the light should be brought vertically downwards again. But few people remember this and just point at the slide.

If you are trembling (and most people are at the beginning of a talk) then the tremor in your hand will be amplified by the laser. Instead of a rock steady point of laser light on the slide there will be a wavering light. If you want to avoid this, try resting the hand holding the laser pointer on the other hand, or rest your arm on your chest or the lectern. This gives the shaky hand a little stability and reduces the movement.

Overhead Projectors

You have to be a certain age to remember being taught using overhead projectors. These were hugely popular in schools, colleges and businesses but have largely been superseded by PowerPoint and computers. OHPs consist of a box, containing a powerful lamp which projects a light which passes through a lens which is focused on a projector screen. The beauty of it is that there are no microprocessors, they are relatively cheap and the slides can be written by hand. The "slides" are actually plastic sheets which are laid onto a stage and the contents of the sheet are projected. Or you can type out the words and project these. Special colored marker pens are use to create the content.

As the speaker goes through the talk he can ask questions of the audience and annotate the transparent sheet as he goes along. This feature is not easy to implement using PowerPoint.

Most organizations have abandoned the use of OHPs but they are still in use in colleges and other educational institutions. Unless you are told you must use an OHP (very unlikely) try to avoid using one.

If you must use the OHP

- Use clean acetate sheets

- If you are writing the content by hand, try to write clearly

- It is better to produce the content on a PC and use acetate sheets compatible with laser printers to produce the material you will be showing

- Keep the stack of acetates in order, to the left of the OHP. Once you have shown a slide, move it to the right and pick up the next sheet

- Number the sheets as well

- Don't block the field of view – stand to one side, away from the screen so the audience can see clearly

Blackboards & Whiteboards

Again, like OHPs these allow spontaneity and free flowing thought, unlike the staid and relatively static PowerPoint slides. You can start with a blank board and as you develop your theme you can note down words, create drawings and diagrams and the audience can watch or can copy down what you are writing.

Blackboards or whiteboards are very useful when you want to start with nothing on the screen and lecture in a style that allows a gradual unfolding of a story. You are much less constrained than when you use computer projection.

Hot tip

If you are teaching a small group, blackboards, whiteboards and flip charts provide a useful way of jotting down ideas. They are not useful with large audiences.

This style would suit a small audience but many universities and colleges have used blackboards for generations of students, even when there are 100 or more in the audience.

At most conference venues blackboards will not be available. Whiteboards are more popular but again, these are not used in large meetings. You are most likely to encounter whiteboards in company meeting rooms.

If you do intend to use this medium for your speech, write slowly and clearly.

If something is not clear, rub it out and write it again. Check that everyone can see the text. If they cannot, write using a larger size.

Prepare For the Worst

Anything that can go wrong will go wrong, is the old adage. And it's true. This is especially so when using highly complex equipment like laptops, AV projectors and the like. We tend to take these for granted but at some point when you are giving a talk, or just about to start, something will go wrong.

Technology failure

Perhaps your memory stick cannot be read. Maybe you have used a Mac and are trying to open PowerPoint on a PC laptop. Bring both PC and Mac formatted drives with the presentation to the meeting. Bring one extra version on another stick in case one becomes corrupted.

Your graphics displayed perfectly on your home computer but do not show correctly at the meeting. Again this may be a Mac/PC issue, or perhaps you have more memory on your home machine than at the conference. You may have used large TIFF files rather than JPEGs for your images (remember, AV projectors only project at 75dpi so there is no need to save your digital images at 600dpi. This only bloats your presentation file and adds nothing to the image that is projected).

The projector may fail, the bulb may blow. This is not your problem and the AV people will need to sort this out. It could hold you up while you wait so it is perhaps best to continue your talk without visuals. Just *ad lib*, and if you have your handout with you check what the next slide would be and discuss it anyway. The audience will be forgiving since they know it's not your fault.

The laser pointer may fail. The AV staff will sort this but meantime, just deliver your talk without pointing things out.

Alarm bells

Fire alarms can go off during your presentation (this actually happened to me recently, presenting to a small group in a hotel). There's little you can do but go with the flow. File out, wait, then come back in. Let the organizers decide what to do next!

The human factor

Your mind may go blank while you present. Sometimes a word eludes you, or a key fact. Just say something like *"Oh well, anyway..."* then move to the next slide or point. Don't make a big deal of it, and the chances are the audience will not notice.

Handouts Are Useful

We all love handouts and feel cheated if we don't get them. The reason they are so useful is because if you don't produce handouts, many audience members will feel compelled to copy the contents of the slides as you go through your presentation and they will not be listening to you. If, on the other hand, you have handouts they will simply add annotations to the handout.

Should your handouts be the same as your slides?

Yes and no. Yes because that is what the audience expects to see. But this means that you could pass round the handout and the audience could leave because everything you are going to say will be printed on the handout. The way it *should* work is that you have fairly simple slides which complement your speech. *You* are the main attraction and they should be listening to you. The slides are an accompaniment and should not be able to stand alone without you. The handouts should be more detailed than your projected slides. You can include graphs and charts that might be useful to the audience but which you do not necessarily wish to cover in your speech. A simple slide deck with complicated handouts allows you to be very flexible in what you say during the presentation since you are not tied to text written on a slide.

In reality, few of us have time to create handouts that differ from the main presentation and if you are going to provide handouts then like most people you will probably just make these a reproduction of your presentation.

Most slide software programs allow you to print handouts in a variety of formats: 2, 4, 6, or 9 slides per sheet. There is also an option to include blank lines for delegates notes. The print dialog box here shows the settings for black and white print with 3 slides per page.

Below are handouts printed at 3 and 6 per page. Note the 3 slide option has lines included so the audience can write their own notes.

Handouts can also be printed in color but this makes them more difficult to read. It also adds to the expense.

Hot tip

Handouts, printed 3 slides to a page are useful for lectures and other situations where you expect the audience to take notes.

Summary

- Some people are skilled at standing up in front of an audience and delivering a great speech with no props at all

- This takes nerve and smart planning

- It focuses the audience's attention entirely on you, since there are no slides, OHP, or blackboard for them to look at

- More commonly presenters use some form of visual aids, often in the form of computer projected slides

- These should contain key elements of your talk but should not act as a major distraction – you still want the audience to focus on *you* and what you are saying

- You can liven up the content of your speech by showing video, either as a standalone feature or within a computer presentation

- Prewritten notes are often used by inexperienced presenters. But rather than serve as a useful resource and support, the scripted notes will make your speech lack spontaneity and the negative feedback you get from the audience will reduce your confidence

- Scripts and prompts such as cards are useful, especially if there is complicated information to discuss

- Microphones are used in larger meetings so that the entire audience can hear what you are saying. Most of us need to be shown how to use these properly

- Highlight information on the screen using a laser pointer but, as with other technology, learn how to use it properly

- Media such as blackboards, OHPs and flip charts are fine for small informal meetings. Learn to write in large letters and make sure your writing is clear

- Handouts are useful for the audience. It means they do not have to write down everything you say. You can make these more detailed than your slides if you want the projected material to be uncluttered. Most people, however, simply make the handout a hard copy of their slide content

6 Getting Ready For the Big Day

As the big day arrives your nerves will be on edge and you will be fearing the worst. It need not be this way. The audience are on your side and want you to succeed. All it needs is some self-belief on your part to make it work.

Clarify Your Goals

Confidence comes from being sure of your material and having a very clear concept of what you are trying to achieve. We have discussed this already in the book but it does no harm to repeat it again. You need to be clear in your own mind what is expected of you when you speak to your audience, and importantly, you need to clarify for yourself what you want the audience to take away from your speech.

For informal gatherings, wedding speeches and the like, this is not too crucial since your role is to entertain and provide a fun speech on the day. You are not providing instruction or trying to sell anything. However, if you are invited to a major business or academic conference you will be speaking as an expert on your topic. You cannot possibly cover the entire area so you must focus on what you think is important. You should have researched the topic and sifted through all the information to identify the real gems that you want the audience to take away.

On a blank page, using the left hand column, try writing down the goals you have been given by the person or organization that invited you to speak. In the right column write down some of the things you feel are most important and, if you could achieve it, what would be the points you would most want your audience to remember from the talk long after the event.

Once you have identified these you are then in a much stronger position to start drafting your speech. Keep these points nearby as you write so that you can be sure you stay focused rather than wander off-topic into areas that are less useful for your speech.

Don't forget

Are your goals crystal clear? If not, work on them now.

Key points

1 We are the best in the business

2 Main threats

2 Strategies to ensure we stay top

Rehearse Your Speech Again

Again, with these points in mind, set aside ample practice time. Go through your slides on paper (the printed handouts) and also on screen, if you are using slides. Using a highlighter pen, go through the printed version and highlight the text, images or other visuals that support your goals.

If you spot anything that seems redundant or obscure you can remove this later.

How does it sound?

When you practice out loud does the speech sound coherent? Does it sound interesting? If you were in the audience, would you personally find this interesting to listen to? Are there areas which are dull or less interesting? You might want to remove these, or rephrase the slide and your spoken message.

- Keep rehearsing right up until the speech itself. This will have numerous benefits

- You will feel in control and will be more confident that your speech will hit the spot and make a major impact

- You will learn your material and, if you are using them, your slides or other visual props

- You will not be fazed when you change slide – you will know exactly why it's there and what to say

- However, you will not be learning the speech verbatim since each time you give it you will use slightly different words so it will sound natural and not scripted

- You will become totally confident in terms of what to say to each slide. There will be little risk of you drying up or forgetting how to address any aspect of your speech

- Your anxiety levels will fall and your ability to concentrate will be improved

- The opposite is true: if you fail to practice your speech you will start to forget what you have included in the speech

- This will make you anxious in case you have forgotten something vital (though when you recheck the speech you often find it was there all along)

Organize Yourself

One way of alleviating anxiety and remaining in control is to be highly organized. The last thing you want to be doing is rushing around the house on the morning of your speech looking for laser pointers, laptop cables and a memory stick to put your speech on.

Make yourself a checklist or use the one on the next page to make sure you have all you need.

Don't forget

Make yourself a list of all the things you need for your speech and cross them off as you deal with each one.

- Travel information if needed (passport, e-ticket, train ticket, hotel details)

- Don't forget to take your wallet and some foreign currency

- Laptop, charger, wireless slide changer, adaptor to connect Mac laptop to AV projector

- USB memory sticks: take 2 or 3, this ensures that if one fails you will have a backup

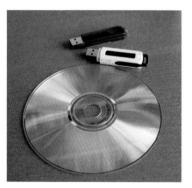

- Burn your presentation onto a CD as well just in case

- Take your own laser pointer and spare batteries in case the one at the meeting does not work or fails part way through

- You might want to upload your talk to a website so that if your briefcase is lost, you can still get hold of a copy of your presentation. Dropbox (*www.getdropbox.com*), MobileMe (*www.me.com*) and other services are useful for this purpose

- Make sure you have saved your presentation in a number of formats. Use an older PowerPoint format as well as the latest in case the laptop at the venue does not have the most recent version of the software installed

- If you are preparing slides on a Mac, try them out on a PC before you leave home to make sure the graphics and transitions work. If they don't, *fix them*

- Make sure you have at least one hard copy of your talk, for example a printed handout which should be annotated with your own notes

- If you have used data or other information from journal articles you might want to take these as well just in case you want to double check the details later

- If you are not using slides, make sure you have your pile of index cards with your speech notes, and have one index card containing just the headings for the main speech

- If you are giving a social speech such as a Best Man's speech, take a copy of the outline of your speech with you, printed in large letters (16 to 18 point) so you can keep this on the table as you speak so that you can see the headings, but avoid reading from it

- Wear a watch with a face that is easy to read so you can time yourself as you give your presentation

- Don't forget to take handkerchiefs and some mints to suck – candy helps keep your mouth from going dry

✓ Travel information

✓ Passport, e-ticket, train ticket.

✓ Hotel details

✓ Laptop & charger

✓ Wireless slide changer

✓ Adaptor to connect Mac laptop to AV projector

✓ USB memory sticks: take 2 or 3

✓ Burn your presentation onto a CD as well just in case

✓ Upload talk to a website

Take presentation in various formats (include older format) ✓

Check presentation on PC ✓

Take printed copy with annotated notes ✓

Take index cards if not using laptop to present ✓

Social speech: take copy of outline ✓

When You Get There

What to do when you get there

Try to get there early. There is nothing worse than rushing into the lecture room with the audience in place waiting for you to speak. Your anxiety level will be very high if you do this.

Have a general look round at the layout of the room. Look at the audience seats. Stand at the lectern, if there is one, and practice looking at the whole room. You will want to engage with the audience throughout your talk so now is a good time to get a feel for what it will be like.

If you spend too much time chatting to colleagues you will leave yourself little time to get organized. Stake your claim on a front row seat, and make sure you are comfortable with the equipment, have loaded your slides, have your water and other items close to hand so that when proceedings start, you are cool, calm and collected. The last thing you want is to be flustered just before you give a speech.

- Get your slides loaded onto the laptop.

- Practice changing slides forward (and back)

- Try out the laser pointer

- Can you see the screen easily from where you will be standing? If not, is there a laptop screen in front of you so you can see the content of the slides?

- Practice using the microphone. Is it fixed (keep facing forward)? Will there be a lapel microphone? This is better since you can move freely without the sound quality being affected

- Can the lights be dimmed a little without you being in total darkness?

- Grab yourself a bottle or glass of water. Quite often our throats dry up (nerves) and a quick drink of water makes things easier

- Have you got a seat near the front? Choose one now, making sure you only have a short walk to the podium

- Keep your notes to hand along with a copy of your handouts so you can familiarize yourself with the content again

Meet the Team

Meet the organizers and the AV technician

These guys know how everything works. It is their job to make sure the slides project, the lighting is correct, and that you have everything you need to give your speech. They will also check sound levels to make sure these are satisfactory.

If you have any technical worries, for example about your slides, check it out with them. They will help make sure the slides project as well as possible. If any formatting changes need to be made they may help with this.

Using your own laptop

Many speakers prefer to use their own laptops and this may be accommodated. However, it is best not to assume you can do this – certainly for larger conferences the organizers will insist on you loading your presentation onto a central computer or server and running the show from there. This is because they want seemless transitions between speakers and prefer not to have speakers unplugging AV cables which can take time.

If you use your own laptop you run the risk that the AV projector will not "see" the input source. Sometimes projector and laptop do not communicate with each other. A reboot may fix this but the audience gets restless while you try to sort out the AV glitches.

Mac users sometimes forget to take the necessary AV cable which is required to hook up to the projector. Mac laptops do not have the correct socket to allow most AV projectors to plug in directly. Instead, you must use a specific adaptor which will either be supplied with the Mac laptop or can be purchased separately.

If you need to show a video from a DVD the AV technicians need to know this. They will likely use a separate computer to run the DVD so you need to tell them when you want the DVD shown, for example, after slide 20. They will then cut from the slide presentation to DVD and when the DVD has ended will switch on the slide presentation once more.

Don't be afraid to ask!

If you have any worries or niggling doubts ask the technical team. They are generally very knowledgeable and will do all they can to make sure things run smoothly. For this reason I cannot stress enough how important it is to be there well ahead of your speech.

Beware

Using your own laptop has advantages but it can cause technical problems. In general it is safer to use the facilities at the venue.

Mingle With the Audience

These are the people we fear, not because they are intrinsically bad, but because we are addressing them in whatever capacity we are speaking. They may be wedding guests, or colleagues from work. Or the audience may be 2,000 international experts attending an annual conference on a highly specialized subject.

Providing you are there early enough, you will be able to meet with the audience as they come into the lecture room. Try to say hello and chat about whatever comes naturally – their business, city, weather, just anything that helps break the ice. They will become human rather than just an amorphous mass

Hot tip

Try to meet some of the audience and introduce yourself before the show starts. It will help to calm you down.

Often, at the time of registration, there will be coffee served and this also provides a great opportunity to meet people.

Carry some business cards in your top jacket pocket. You never know when you might need one and if someone offers you theirs you feel foolish if you don't have yours to exchange with them.

Above all, try not to be shy. After all, you will soon be the main attraction and all eyes will be on you so engage with them now! You will be amazed at how much better you will feel after you have chatted to a few people before you give your talk. Rather than the "unknown", they become friends and this will help later on when you face them from the stage.

Calm Yourself Down

Anxiety just before giving a speech is always high. This is the time when we fear we will have omitted key information, or that our talk will be substandard.

But if you have practiced extensively you will know that your speech is great and so there's no need to worry about not delivering a killer presentation.

Scan through your handout while you wait to speak. This will refresh your memory about your speech and help reduce the fear level.

Strategy for inner calm

- Keep thinking positive thoughts. Imagine what it will be like to give this great speech. Imagine, also, the feeling when you have finished and have sat down. Think of the applause you will receive

- Remember, too, that *you* have been asked to give this speech. The other hundreds or possibly thousands in the room have not. You are the expert and this is recognition of that fact. You know much more than they do and they will be looking up to you to teach them and inform them

- Try taking some deep breaths and stretch a little to get rid of any built-up tension

- Turn your head slowly, fully, from side to side. Get rid of any knots in your muscles

- Have a drink of water

- Flick through your notes or handout. Remind yourself of the first few opening lines

- If you can, try to listen to the talks before yours. Quite often this is difficult since our thoughts are racing and we are so focused on our own talks. But listening to someone else's presentation takes your mind off things and may even make you feel better if their talk is not all that great

- As far as possible try not to have negative thoughts about *"What if it goes badly"*, *"I hope I haven't used too many slides"*, since these only make you feel worse at a time when you are vulnerable

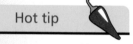

Hot tip

Try to get yourself as relaxed as possible (under the circumstances) – this will enhance your performance.

Visit the Restroom

We generally feel like we need to visit the bathroom more frequently before stressful events. The adrenaline rushing around

our bloodstream causes this, and we all get it at times of stress. Quite often the simple act of going out and having a change of air can energize you and make you feel much better by the time you come back.

Don't forget

Visit the restroom before you speak and fix your appearance if anything appears to be out of place.

- It doesn't matter if you don't really need to go, but go anyway

- Wash your hands, and splash water on your face

- Straighten your tie or clothes

- Take some more big breaths

- Check your teeth and hair. Is anything out of place? Fix it

- Check your shoes are clean

- Make sure you have some tissues in your pocket in case your nose starts to run (but don't start wiping your brow with it! This sends out the wrong signals)

- Walk slowly back to the room, still taking the occasional very deep breath

- Practice your opening sentences as you go (not out loud) just to be absolutely sure you know what you are going to say the minute you start to speak

- Try to stretch as many muscles as possible on the way back to lessen the tension even more. Walk briskly back to get the circulation going, and try to shake your arms as well (providing no-one is watching you!)

Start With Confidence

You may not be looking forward to getting up there but you need to *look* like you are. You are so happy to be invited up on the stage to talk, and you couldn't imagine being anywhere else. This is a great opportunity. Show it by smiling (not grimacing) as you walk up to the lectern.

● Try to walk briskly to the podium, lectern or wherever you are expected to stand – avoid shuffling, or walking too slowly

● Give the impression of confidence and calmness, and keep smiling!

● Look out at the audience before you start. Take in all sides, and avoid just looking at the people immediately in front of you

● Thank the chairman, if there is one, or whoever has just introduced you to the audience

● Take off your watch and lay it down so you can see the time. Note when you are starting so you can keep to time

● Place your notes in front of you if you are using these and make sure you can see them clearly

● Is the title slide on the screen? Can you see it well enough? If not, you might want to move to a position where you can see it

Your first few words

We will cover the introductory sentences in Chapter 8. These first few moments are critical to the success or failure of a speech. If you can get this bit right, you are more or less home and dry.

As you start to speak you will find your voice. You can gauge how loudly or quietly you must speak in order to be heard. You may have a microphone and even though you practiced before the session, you could not be entirely sure what it would sound like for real. Now you do.

If you were to stumble through the first couple of slides and sentences you would be feeling more anxious, since you would fear the whole speech would be like this. You would know that the audience will be judging you and a shaky start does not bode well for the rest of the speech. However, if you appear confident

and comfortable in this situation and your first few sentences are word perfect, and delivered at the correct pace, you will have their interest.

Slick opening statement

It helps to practice any speech but the opening section needs more work than the main part of the talk.

Get your title and affiliation perfect – "*I'm John Doe from The Ford Motor Company and I am going to talk about our latest model*". Then go to the next slide. "*In this talk I will be discussing X, Y and Z. Let's begin with Y...*". Write down exactly what you will say about slide Y. You do not need to memorize this but you do need a clearly written piece of text that captures what you want to say.

Write down or type into your word processor what you will say to this slide and perhaps one or two slides after that. This will take you through the introduction and the main body of the speech.

Read and re-read these opening words. Don't change the words now or when you give the talk since it will throw you off and you will forget what comes next.

Try not to make it sound scripted and don't read from a script. If you have gone over it several times you should recall what you must say.

Once you have managed to get through the first part of your speech you will have gained the audience's attention and you should be feeling better and more relaxed.

The rest of the talk will be familiar to you since you should have practiced many times before you got to this stage.

The final part of your speech, where you conclude, should ram home the key points. These are critical to get right. You want to leave the audience with a simple message, so use only a few points at the end to sum up the entire presentation.

They will forget most of what you said but you want to leave them remembering that you were a great speaker and you also want them to recall your summary, the key points or the learning points in an educational lecture. The bit in the middle is important but the beginning and end are the critical sections.

Summary

- Mental and physical preparation are important if you want to perform well and deliver a great speech

- Go over your goals again. Are these still crystal clear? If you are using slides, have you got your messages clearly stated at the end of the presentation?

- Keep rehearsing right up until the day of the speech. You cannot practice too much

- Make a checklist of things you must take with you to the meeting. If you are not using any props then this will be less of a worry

- If you are using computer slides, you will need to make sure you have your presentation saved on a memory stick or two (and CD ROM). Make sure you have saved in the most "popular" (often an older) version of the presentation software, such as PowerPoint. Using the package released this week will definitely fail unless you are projecting from your own laptop

- If you are traveling, make sure you have your passport, e-ticket and any other information needed for the journey

- Take a hard copy of your presentation, preferably one annotated with your own notes so you can refer to these before the talk

- Arrive early at the venue and get your slides loaded onto their PC or laptop

- Familiarize yourself with the other AV equipment such as microphone, slide changer and laser pointer before you give your speech – this saves the embarrassment of not knowing how to use it when standing in front of an audience

- Facing the audience can be daunting so try to reduce the anxiety by meeting some of them over coffee at registration time or while you are waiting for proceedings to begin

- Try to take deep breaths and calm yourself down before your speech. Make one last visit to the restroom and adjust your tie and make sure your appearance is up to scratch

7 Looking the Part

Audiences are judgemental.

They will decide whether

they like you within the first

few minutes of your pitch.

Dress well and boost your

inner confidence.

Hot tip

The audience's first impressions are critical. They will decide very quickly whether or not they like you. Do your utmost to make a great initial impression.

First Impressions

Your audience will decide within the first few minutes of your speech whether they like you or not. Many studies have shown this and there's no getting away from it. If you make an initial bad impression it is very difficult to get them to "like" you if you fail to impress initially.

For this reason it is critical that your entrance is confident, you engage the audience right from the start, and your first few sentences are solid.

There are many factors which contribute to the initial first impressions. Partly it will be based on what you look like. Have you made an effort to dress well? This would show consideration for your role in the proceedings. It will let them know that you are taking this seriously and are catering for them, the audience (remember, this is about *them* and not you).

They will watch the way you walk, position yourself at the lectern or wherever you are speaking, they will be watching to see if you make eye contact with them or whether you stare down at your notes. If you are at ease and start well they will relax.

On the other hand, if you appear tense and tentative they will be on edge and will not relax.

Although they do want you to succeed, audiences can be a little unforgiving at times.

Key elements to looking slick and being liked are:

- Look good

- Be confident

- Smile

- Appear happy to be there

- Acknowledge them by surveying the whole room

- Start your speech confidently, with no apologies or stumbling through the content

- Be yourself as much as possible – do not affect a different accent or voice (this will sound unnatural)

- Keep smiling wherever possible

Rescue Me!

Sometimes, no matter how well you plan, things go wrong. Some will be your fault and some may be no-one's fault. If this happens at the beginning of your speech you are likely to feel devastated and looking for the nearest trap-door to jump through and escape!

Don't panic

Easier said than done. Sometimes your heart is really thumping just before you get on stage. You can hardly think and as you try to thank your host, hardly any sound comes out. Stop!

Don't just try to carry on – take a sip of water (you did remember to take a glass of water up with you, right?). Swallow the water, take a deep breath and start to speak. The chances are your heart rate will have slowed and you can continue.

Glitches

- Your presentation may fail to load – ask the AV guys to help here. The same is true for any system failure that involves the equipment

- Your mouth dries up a few minutes into your pitch – have a drink of water

- You stutter or stammer – slow down. Your brain is racing ahead and your mouth cannot keep up. Slowing yourself down – *consciously* – helps

- You get someone's name wrong or use the wrong word somewhere – just correct it and move on. Don't dwell on it or highlight it. The chances are the audience won't notice

- You lose your thread – sometimes this happens. You are talking on a topic, get yourself side tracked, then forget where you are actually meant to be in the presentation. If you are really lost just move to the next slide and things will be back on track once more

What to Wear

This is not a beauty contest so you do not have to go out and spend thousands of dollars on designer outfits. You should generally try to appear smartly dressed. The better dressed you are the more likely the audience is to take you seriously.

Men

For men this would usually mean wearing a dark suit, with a light colored shirt (white is most neutral) and a smart tie. Shoes should be business shoes or at least smart shoes. If the meeting is "smart casual" you could simply wear chinos and an open necked shirt.

Women

Women have more choice in clothes but in general should stick to business style attire with dark suit or jacket and skirt. Try to avoid garish colors or large bold stripes. As a general rule of thumb try to wear the same sort of clothes as you would for a job interview. Stick to shoes with a low heel rather than stilettoes.

If you are very eminent you could probably wear a tee shirt and jeans. Or you could be like Steve Jobs and wear a black turtleneck sweater and jeans but since he is CEO of the company he can pretty much wear what he wants. There is a TED (*www.ted.com*) video of James Watson, who discovered the structure of DNA many years ago, giving a talk looking very casual. Sadly most of us are not in their league so it is best to be conventional!

Maybe you are worried about being too smartly dressed, while the audience is in tee shirts and jeans. That's fine, don't worry. It gives you a position of authority and control. They are far more likely to listen to you than if you were dressed very casually.

For weddings and other social gatherings wear outfits appropriate to the occasion.

Don't forget

Do spend some time deciding what to wear. Try to look business-like and smart.

Buying New Outfits

It is tempting to buy new clothes for your speech. If you are to give a number of speeches you could end up with an enormous wardrobe! New clothes often make us feel more confident which is no bad thing. In addition, old suits, jackets or skirts may look fine for working day to day but may look slightly tired. This gives out signals to the audience who will expect you to look crisp and well turned out.

If you want to splash out on a new business suit, that's fine but make sure it fits right and feels comfortable before the big day. Make sure you unpick the sticking that holds the pockets together and remember to take the stitched label off the sleeve if there is one. A mid-price suit, well-tailored, will make the audience take notice and they are more likely to be persuaded by you than if you wear something old.

If you are wearing new shoes, wear them round the house to break them in a bit. Shoes often feel fine for the first couple of minutes. You throw them in your suitcase, wear them at the conference and find out after 10 minutes that they are agony to wear! Don't forget to take the price tag off the bottom before you give your speech.

For men, try to buy a new tie that is not too jazzy and colorful. Buy a decent quality tie with a pattern but colors that are muted.

When buying shirts the safest bet is to go for something white with standard collar (not button down) or you could wear pale blue. Avoid bold stripes and checks. Classic lines in suit, shirt, tie and shoes is always safest and most conventional.

Any Bad Habits?

Beware

Bad habits detract from even a great speech. Work out what yours are and deal with them.

Do you have any bad habits?

We all have them and you may know what yours are. When you give a speech you want nothing to distract the audience from the content of your pitch.

As listeners, the things that annoy us are:

- People who say "um" and "er" a lot as they speak

- Playing with your hair or beard

- Adjusting your spectacles constantly

- Lack of eye contact with the audience

- Reading from a script either fully for the whole speech or parts of your speech

- Talking in a monotonous pitch throughout

- Forgetting to pause and talking in a continuous stream

- Talking too fast

- Pacing around like a caged animal

- Playing with jewelry or coins in your pockets

- Playing with a pen, popping the top off and on

- Keeping your hands in your pockets

- Waving the laser pointer all over the place

- Waving arms around or moving around the stage too much

Once you have identified your bad habits you can start working on these. It's not too difficult to sort once you know what the problem is.

Record Yourself Speaking

It is never easy to watch yourself on video or listen to yourself. *"Do I really sound like that?"* It's hard to believe but what we hear through our ears obviously differs to what the audience hears as the recording will attest! Nonetheless, you do sound like that. But the important thing is to record yourself – ask a colleague to video you when you give your next lecture or deliver your next speech. Watch yourself carefully (ignore the sound for now – in fact, switch off the audio). Do you look natural? Are you doing anything likely to annoy people in the audience watching? Make a note of the offending bad habits so you can work on these later.

Next, try to listen to the audio content. How do you sound? Masterful? Nervous? Are you managing to vary the pitch as you go through your talk? Or are you talking in a monotone?

By watching and listening to yourself you can start to address the problems associated with your delivery style. Even if you are a seasoned presenter, there may still be one or two aspects you could improve to make yourself even more slick.

If you can't bear to watch yourself or listen to the audio ask a colleague to provide honest feedback after your next speech.

Listening on the move
Recording yourself is actually a great way to rehearse and run through your entire speech. When you have made the recording, save it in a format which can be synced to an MP3 player such as an iPod. When you are in the car, underground or just walking around you can play your speech over and over. This will really help embed it in your brain!

Hot tip

Recording yourself giving your speech has many advantages. You can hear what you actually sound like, it helps you pace your speech, and you can burn it to CD or MP3 player for listening to on the move.

Keep Hands Out of Pockets!

Why do we always want to stick our hands in our jacket pockets when we stand up to speak? This is very common and happens to even very experienced presenters. Maybe it's because we want to appear relaxed or maybe we don't know where to put our hands.

There must be something we can do with our hands to avoid the slovenly look it gives to just stick them in a pocket!

Try placing one hand on the lectern and use one hand to hold the laser pointer. Or you could clasp your hands in front of you while you talk and every now and then use one to point things out or gesticulate.

Some people have very expressive hands – watch politicians or senior world leaders when they talk. They use their hands a great deal but not in a distracting or annoying way.

They use their hands as a means of driving home their message. See if you can incorporate some of their hand movements in your own speeches.

Don't wave your hands around excessively while you talk. The audience will watch your hands and not listen to what you are saying.

Where to Stand?

Stand behind the podium or move around the stage?

Your positioning says much about how confident you are when you give your speech. Consciously or otherwise we use the podium or lectern in different ways depending on our experience and confidence level. Your ability to leave the safety of the lectern reflects your overall confidence.

The inexperienced person will move to the lectern and cling on to the sides using the lectern almost as a flotation device, never leaving the safety of the support. In effect, if you deliver your speech this way you are hiding from the audience or using the lectern as a barrier separating yourself from the audience.

Although this sounds bad, this practice is widespread in universities and academic conferences. It would be unusual for a speaker in a medical conference to wander all over the stage. Sometimes this is because the microphone is fixed and the speaker simply has to remain at the lectern, but more often it is because the convention is simply to stand behind the lectern and deliver your presentation from that position.

The lectern is a barrier

The lectern provides a definite buffer or barrier between you and the audience. It does feel more comfortable standing behind a wooden structure than it does to be in the middle of the stage where we feel more vulnerable and exposed.

There is a risk that you will disappear altogether if you have a darkened room with a lectern off to one side and you are behind it. If you are using slides these will dominate and all eyes will be on the slides rather than you. This has definite advantages (takes the heat off you) and disadvantages (they can't see you, so you could almost just prerecord your speech and play that while showing the slides).

So there is no absolute right or wrong here. The way you deliver your speech depends on the circumstances, your confidence or comfort level and normal convention. If you try to do something that is not natural to you or the occasion you risk something going wrong. Find your own comfort level, and build your confidence using that. Once you are more experienced try doing something different and see how that works.

Beware

The lectern may feel like a place of safety but it also creates a barrier between you and your audience. If you can, try to move away – at least every now and again.

Look 'Em in the Eye

Face the audience and make eye contact

Turning your back on the audience is one of the cardinal sins of presenting. There are many very experienced presenters who address mainly their slides. They put their elbow on the lectern, face the slides and talk through these and point things as out as they go using the laser. Why is that bad? The information is accurate, and they are highlighting the things they want us to know, yet it is annoying to watch a presentation like that. In general when we are talking one-on-one or to a small group we converse with them. We face them and chat to them. They feel involved in the discussion. When a speaker turns his or her back they have disengaged with the audience and so we, as the audience, no longer feel involved. We are passively watching a show just as we would with TV. Yet this is a live person so why is he not looking at us and involving us?

Turning your back on the audience is never a good strategy. Just don't do it.

- If you need to read the material that closely you obviously haven't practiced much (which is disrespectful to the audience)

- If you do need reminders of what is on every slide look at the laptop screen which is usually at the lectern. At least that way you keep facing the front which is marginally better. But again, if you know your material you will not need to keep staring at the screen

- Facing the audience, however large, makes them feel that you are talking to them, and involving them even if there is no direct interaction between you and them. Facing the audience and talking to them is part of the engagement that makes good speakers popular

Project Your Personality

"We have nothing to fear but fear itself" – Franklin D. Roosevelt

You are not a robot, nor are you expected to give your speech in a robotic way so try to be natural. If you are a lively person make your speech lively. Use lots of voice intonation and get the audience excited. If the subject of your speech is one you are passionate about try to get that across when you speak.

If you are a very shy and private person you may not enjoy being in the limelight and you may come across as aloof or disinterested. If this is the way you give your speeches you will need to work our a strategy that will help you project yourself or you will find the audience feedback will be poor. This will probably make you withdraw even more into yourself and you will never improve your technique.

You will probably just have to accept that some major change has to be made and work on it. Make yourself more outgoing (at least when you are on the stage). It may feel unnatural at first but you can build on it and improve.

Get networking
To be a confident speaker you are going to have to find ways of overcoming your natural reticence. You need to look for opportunities to speak.

Volunteer
Why not put yourself forward as a speaker either internally, perhaps presenting data to your work colleagues as part of a regular departmental meeting, or if you know someone who is organizing a meeting why not ask to be on the speaker list?

Yes it's scary and it's understandable that this is the last thing you would want to do.

But do you know what? Most things we dread are *not* that scary. Most of our fears are unfounded and we are frightened of what we *imagine* it might be like. What if this happens? Or that happens? It is all speculative. The chances are, once you've done it you will get a real buzz and say *"It wasn't that bad after all!"*.

Having got through this one why not volunteer for more? The experiences are additive and eventually you will not fear any speaking event again!

Know When to Shut Up

Many people, when anxious, try to fill every second of the time they are on the stage, or giving their speech. They seem to hardly take a breath but keep going relentlessly like a runaway train that eventually stops leaving us breathless too.

Pacing yourself is difficult and has to be a very conscious decision. Watch TV presenters reading the news. They do not talk in a constant stream going from story to story without a break. They use multiple techniques to make their delivery interesting. They vary the speed of their speech, they change intonation, posing questions, making statements, and they introduce pauses.

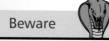
The most important place to pause is when moving from one aspect of a speech to another. The pause need only be 1 or 2 seconds but this will feel like a long time when you are the presenter. Try it the next time you give a talk. As you go from one slide to another, or one topic to another pause for a second or so and just look at the audience. It will appear like a pregnant pause, very poignant and it may even appear dramatic or uncomfortable.

This is a great technique to use if you want them to take special note of what you have just said. You deliver the points you think are important, wait, and then move on to the next item. This will make them sit up and take notice. Obviously you would not use this for every slide or important point but you could introduce it if there are areas you really want them to remember.

The other area where we tend to let our mouths run away with us comes during the Question and Answer session. If we are a little anxious, we try to answer the question but we often keep talking even when we've answered it! *Just stop!* Make the answer as long as it needs to be to answer the question then stop. This allows for more questions to be asked and will increase your popularity with the audience.

- Always avoid giving the audience unnecessary detail such as saying what time you caught the train to get here, or detailing everyone who attended a meeting you were at. This is just not interesting and the audience will switch off!

- Avoid always qualifying information or your opinions. For example, saying things like "*I think this is very important ... but you probably won't*" will make you sound indecisive. Never apologize during a speech, if you can avoid it

- Try to avoid offending your audience. Steer clear of topics – humorous or otherwise – that are political or sexual or offensive in other ways. This does not go down well with audiences

- Again, much of this comes with practice and experience. Eventually you will give a crisp answer and then point to someone with their hand up and say "*Next question?*"

- During Question and Answer sessions, if you feel you are on a roll there is a temptation to give another mini lecture as part of your answer. *Don't.* Just answer the question and take another

- If you reach a section in your talk that has already been covered elsewhere (for example, if someone has asked a question relating to that topic earlier) do not go through the whole thing again even if you have taken time to create a slide for it. They have heard it, so move on

- Bear in mind that the more you say, the more ammunition you give people to shoot you down

- If you are not 100% confident talking about a specific aspect either avoid it or keep it very brief. If questioned on it say little. Do not make anything up. Someone in the room may know more than you

- If you are presenting to a small group, read the signals. Do they seem bored or do they look like they can't get enough of what you're saying? If they are glazing over ask them "*Do you want me to skip this bit? Or shall I go through the details?*" See what they say and take your cue from that

Summary

- Giving a speech is a performance and the audience will judge you

- They will see you first, then hear you second

- Audiences generally decide within the first couple of minutes whether or not they like you

- If you make a bad impression at the start it is difficult to recover from this

- Being smartly dressed seldom fails. Try to keep one or two outfits specifically for public speaking engagements

- Wear clothes in which you feel comfortable and confident

- Buy new clothes, by all means, but try them out at least once before the big day – this helps make sure they really fit and also reduces the chance of forgetting to take the labels off shoes, jackets and other items

- We all have bad habits. Some minor irritations can become major if they are repeated 100 times during a speech

- If you are not sure what your bad habits are ask a colleague

- Alternatively, video yourself and watch it critically

- Knowing how and where to stand comes with practice. Most people stay in a safe zone, behind the lectern, throughout their speeches

- This may be necessary, for example, if a fixed podium microphone is being used

- If you are using a lapel microphone, try to move around the stage a little – this makes any presentation less boring

- Try to engage the audience. Look at their faces, and make it feel as though you are talking to them – *personally*

- Project your personality if possible. It is also worth being "larger than life" after all, this is a performance

- You may be on a roll, and could talk for hours but learn when to stop talking

8 Delivery

Public speaking shares many features with amateur dramatics. You need to be larger than life, use some theatrical tricks to impress the audience. By observing your body language and working hard to eliminate any bad habits you can raise your game from mediocre presenter to brilliant presenter!

All the World's a Stage

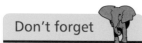

Don't forget

Public speaking is a performance, like any other. Use acting techniques to make you larger than life and really entertain the crowd.

When we give a talk, lecture, or speech we are performing to an audience in much the same way as an actor would. There are many features in common between acting and delivering a speech. The speech has to be written and rehearsed, the event will be publicized and the audience will have much anticipation about the performance. You will dress up for the occasion and deliver your lines like an actor in a stage play.

As part of the planning for your speech, talk, or lecture you need to think about the role you are expected to, or want to, play. For example, a barrister making submissions to a Judge in court is adopting and *acting out* a markedly different role than a stand-up comic.

Just like any actor, you need to get into character. Before you get up on the stage you need to *think yourself* into the part of the expert, the CEO, or whatever in order to play your part (and deliver your message) well. Getting into character can be done as you wait your turn to speak, or when you visit the restroom before you give your speech.

You should also be larger than life since this will make your speech more interesting. You should practice speaking with more volume than you would normally use. You should introduce the pauses mentioned earlier to heighten the dramatic effect. You should use your hands to make yourself more expressive (without waving them around madly).

In short, speaking in public is an act and you need to play the part if you are going to do it well. You need to get "into character" when you deliver a speech and be larger than life so you can entertain, inform, stimulate and motivate your audience.

"Make sure you have finished speaking before your audience has finished listening." – Dorothy Sarnoff

Relax and be Yourself

This is definitely more easily said than done. Relaxation and giving speeches do not go together! But you do need to loosen up if you are to deliver a convincing performance. If you are totally uptight and rigid with fear you will not be persuasive and you will make the audience feel tense.

How can you possibly relax at a time like this? Some aspects will already have been covered before this stage. The less frightened you are, the more likely you are to feel at ease with the task in hand. If you have planned your speech carefully, and rehearsed extensively you should be pretty much in control of the material and the visuals. The main aspect which is making you nervous now is knowing you have to stand in front of a group of people and talk to them. There is always a large "unknown" component to any public speaking event. Often, you don't know exactly how many will be in the audience, or who they will be (unless you are speaking at a wedding or social event when you should know more or less who will be there), or what the room looks like. You won't have used this laptop or projection screen before and you may have built this up in your mind to be something scary. But if you get to the venue early, as we discussed earlier, you will have had a good look round the room, and tried out the microphone and laptop well in advance. You will have seen the seats so will be able to gauge roughly how many people will attend. Finally, if you meet some of the audience as they arrive or over coffee during registration much of your fear should be allayed.

With a large audience it may be helpful to focus your attention on two or three people across the room, rather than the whole audience but try not to make them feel persecuted by looking *just* at them. Also, try to pick your chosen few from all parts of the audience, not just three people near to you in the front row! This will make them feel uneasy and the rest of the audience may feel left out.

Your first couple of public speaking events will nonetheless be anxious affairs and you are likely to feel tense. Any feeling of being relaxed is likely to come right at the end of the speech.

However, after you have given a few talks you will start to relax much earlier in the proceedings which will improve your delivery considerably since you will start to add pauses, and use your voice in a more theatrical manner to make your speeches more entertaining as well as informative.

Simulate a One-On-One

A public speech to one individual is easy but difficult at the same time. It is easy because you can gauge their response to what you say. They can interact with you, and you can interact with them. You will introduce pauses naturally in order to make sure they have understood what you have just said. With a large audience this is much more difficult to achieve but you can still generate the intimacy and closeness of a one-on-one conversation if you use a conversational approach to your delivery.

Obviously this depends on you, and whether you are comfortable doing this, but when you give a talk to even a very large audience try to introduce phrases or intonation that makes it sound as though you are talking to a small group or one person. Perhaps adding phrases like "*Does that make sense?*"

Try interacting with the group. For example, asking direct questions of the audience such as "*Have you found...?*", "*Does it not always seem that ... happens?*" After asking the question, wait for a short time to register their response to your question, exactly as you would in a one-on-one.

Try pointing to someone in the room and say "*I can see you agree with me.*" or "*I can see you have had the same experience.*"

Clues and cues

It is important to look for, and react to, cues from your audience. If you make a point which appears to exercise the whole audience it is always good to acknowledge the feelings in the room.

Sometimes when we "lecture" we deliver our pitch unaware that we are boring the audience, or saying things with which they disagree. Keep scanning the faces to make sure their feelings are in alignment with yours.

How can you tell?

If they smile and you can see lots of nods it means their views accord with yours. If you say something which generates frowns or people turn to the person next to them and start talking, perhaps pointing at you or your slides, it probably means they disagree with what you are saying. You could try saying "*I am sensing that you don't agree with this? I am happy to stop here and discuss further. Does anyone have strong feelings against this, or wish to comment?*".

Hot tip

You will really engage with the audience if you can simulate a conversation. It takes practice but once you can do this, the audience will warm to you much more.

Get Off to a Good Start

We covered this in the last chapter but it is worth repeating here. The first few minutes of your presentation will set the tone for the whole event. If you start strongly, and appear confident, the chances are your presentation will go well.

How to maximize the first impressions the audience have of you

- Appear confident

- Walk briskly to the podium, lectern or wherever you are speaking

- Smile (difficult, but do try)

- Plan your first few sentences. Write them on a card if need be so you can review them in the days before the talk, and immediately before you give your speech

- You could learn the first couple of sentences if you feel that would help, provided you make it sound natural

Try:
"*Thanks, John/Chairman/whoever, for the kind invitation to speak today. I am honored to be here to be able to talk to you today about our new project. We have some very exciting data that I would like to share with you. In this presentation, which will take about 20 minutes, I will take you through some of the recent work we have been doing and I will outline our plans for the coming year*" – advance from the title slide to the first slide – then begin your speech proper.

If you are speaking to a very large audience, perhaps as part of a conference you might say "*Mr Chairman, Ladies and Gentlemen, I am delighted to be here today to talk to you about…*" or "*My name is John Doe and I am Senior Project Manager for X, and I have been invited to talk to you today about…*".

Or try "*Wow, great introduction. Thanks. I just hope I can live up to your expectations!*" The audience would generally laugh here.

The first couple of sentences are where you find your voice and get a feel for what it's like to talk using the microphone. You will be better able to gauge how far away your head should be from the microphone in order to amplify your voice and it will help ease you in to the main part of the talk.

Using Notes

Notes are not scripts

Notes and scripts are different things. There is no shame in using notes when you deliver a speech. You will have made lots of notes when you were putting your speech together.

A *script* is essentially text that you follow, word for word. This is fine for a sermon where you are expected to deliver a passage verbatim, or a wedding when the vows are taken, but not for a speech. Scripts make you sound stilted and should not be used.

Hopefully you will have made some very succinct notes later during the preparation phase and you may have written these on index cards, or perhaps you used a computer.

If you want to take notes up with you to the lectern when you give your talk there are a few dos and don'ts:

Hot tip

Notes are useful for planning and for rehearsing. Annotate your handouts with written comments or use the Notes feature in your slide software if you are using slides.

120

- Make your notes very brief

- Make sure they are in sequence with the presentation

- Try not to include too much text – stick to key words that will help you remember where you are and what you want to say. Excess text will force you to read, which will be obvious to the audience

- Write on paper or cards using large letters so you can see them even when the lights are dimmed

- Do not hold them in front of you when you speak but try to place them on the lectern (if there is one) so you can discreetly glance down to make sure you have not missed anything out

- Highlight specific important items by circling them or marking with a highlighter pen – these are facts that you cannot forget or, if you do remember to mention them you must be totally accurate. This would include financial information and other data

- Avoid relying too heavily on the notes feature of the popular presentation packages such as PowerPoint or Keynote since these are only of major value if you use your own laptop and can access the Presenter View (where the notes are visible). For most conferences the view you have will be the same as the audience, i.e. just the slides. You could, however, set up your Notes View to use 18 or 20 point font, type in your notes then print off your presentation specifying "Notes View" in the print dialog box. That way you will have a hard copy of your notes pages which will save you rewriting them

Annotating Word's notes pages

Below are two pages printed off using Word's Notes View. Typed notes have been added. In addition, I have annotated the notes with handwritten text. Writing by hand on your notes helps certain key words and facts stand out from the printed text.

All presentation programs have this feature and it doesn't matter which one you use. I have used Microsoft PowerPoint because this program is used for presentation design more than any other.

Printing off in the notes in this format lets you see an image of the slide as well as your notes. If you use only the bottom half of the page you cannot be completely sure which slide the notes refer to.

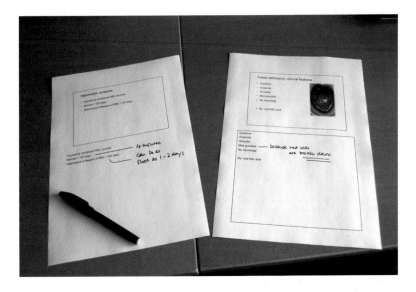

The trick when using this type of notes is to make sure that once you have changed slide, you move the notes sheet to the bottom of the pile, or to the left side so you can see what's on the next sheet. You do not want to get the sheets out of order or you will look anything but slick as you try to regain your composure!

Scripts

These are best used by actors or people on TV reading an autocue or radio presenters. Actors will learn the script by heart and be expected to deliver more or less verbatim. TV presenters will be reading the autocue which is directly under the camera so it will appear as though they are staring straight into the camera even when they are not. On the radio no-one can see you so it doesn't really matter if you use a script.

Delivering a speech using a script makes the speech very dull and, well, scripted. The signals it gives out are that here is a presenter who is so anxious or unsure of himself or herself, that he or she needs to read from a printed script, with little or no spontaneous speech.

I have heard of speakers who not only use a script, but put the script onto PowerPoint slides which they have then shown to the audience. On one occasion the audience started reading aloud too, accompanying the speaker.

Can you ever use a script? I would say that for most of us, giving speeches such as lectures, at conferences, weddings, parties, leaving events and other occasions it is never good to read from a script.

Below is an example of a script that you might use as Best Man at a wedding. The text was typed into a word processor and the font used was Orator. This produces large letters much like the autocue used by President Kennedy in the 1960s.

The text is easy to read but should be used at a large font size so you can lay it on the table and still read it.

You can find many model speech templates online.

LADIES AND GENTLEMEN; BRIDE AND GROOM.

MAY I FIRST SAY THAT THE BRIDESMAIDS ARE LOOKING ABSOLUTELY SMASHING TODAY (WINKS AND POINTS TO ONE IN A FLIRTATIOUS YET FUNNY WAY), AND, ONLY RIGHTLY SO, SECOND TO NONE TO OUR LOVELY BRIDE, MARY. I'M SURE YOU WILL ALL AGREE WITH ME THERE.

FOR THOSE OF YOU WHO DON'T KNOW ME, MY NAME IS JOE BLOGGS, A LONG TIME FRIEND OF JOHN'S. I'VE KNOWN JOHN FOR 20 YEARS; EVER SINCE WE WERE IN KINDERGARTEN TOGETHER. SINCE THEN, WE HAVE HAD MANY EPIC ADVENTURES TOGETHER: FROM RUNNING AWAY FROM SCHOOL, RUNNING FROM THE POLICE, BAR BRAWLS, WOMEN AND TRIPS AROUND THE WORLD. SO THE TIME WE HAVE SPENT TOGETHER MEANS THAT TOM HAS, IN A WAY, SHAPED MY SENSE OF HUMOUR - SO IF YOU FIND THIS SPEECH RATHER UNFUNNY, YOU CAN BLAME HIM.

ETC…

Cue Cards

These are similar to notes. Index cards or similar small cards can be used to write (in large bold letters) subheadings or prompts for you to use as you go through your speech. Once you have written these, have them arranged in order of appearance so you do not have to fumble around to find the right card.

Once you have used one cue card, place it to one side or on the bottom of the pile so you do not inadvertently use it again.

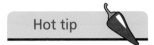

Hot tip

Cue cards are useful to keep you on track but keep them simple so you can see the content at a glance.

Cue cards can be made easily by printing off your talk (using PowerPoint or Keynote handout mode) then going through with a yellow highlighter pen to pick out items that will act as useful cues as you go through your presentation.

If your printer takes envelopes you could set up a template for your index cards and feed these through the printer if your handwriting is not good enough to be read easily when you are giving your talk.

Cue cards for informal occasions

Cue cards may well be the best aide memoires for more informal speeches, such as a Best Man's speech or the Groom's speech at a wedding, as an alternative to the printed sheet (shown on the facing page). Cue cards are useful at events when it would be inappropriate to use more formal methods such as a laptop presentation or a formal script.

Cue cards are also cheap, easy to edit wherever you are, recyclable, do not require power and they are highly portable!

> *I have a dream that one day this nation will rise up and live out the true meaning of its creed: "We hold these truths to be self-evident: that all men are created equal."*
>
> Martin Luther King, 1963

Thank the Organizers

Don't forget to thank the organizers for inviting you to talk

Just as you are polite and respectful to the audience, it is also customary to thank whoever invited you to speak in the first place. You will need to phrase this to suit the occasion.

It is during the first minute or two that we are most anxious and the first words we speak will be to say *Thank You*. So you want to focus your energies on getting this right.

A large formal meeting would warrant the type of thank you mentioned earlier:

- *"Mr Chairman, Ladies & Gentlemen..."*

- *"Mr Chairman, colleagues..."*

- *"It is an honor and a privilege to be asked to speak at today's session on X..."*

- *"I was delighted to be asked to take part in this year's ..."*

If the occasion is informal or internal then you don't really need to thank your work colleagues but you could just say *"Thanks, John, okay, today I want to focus on..."*.

Acting as principal speechmaker

If you are acting as the principal speechmaker at an informal gathering, it is always respectful to acknowledge and thank those who have provided the hospitality on behalf of all those present.

You may need to co-ordinate the toasts on behalf of the whole audience. If this is likely, it is essential for you to ensure that drinks are provided in advance, for the toasts.

Don't forget

It is polite to thank whoever invited you to speak but keep it short.

124

Watch Your Body Language

Again, this is all about performance and avoiding subconscious behaviors which may not be obvious to you but will be read by the audience. Failing to smile, arms crossed as you speak or take questions, frowning or shaking your head if someone says something during the Question & Answer with which you disagree, pointing at people, shrugging your shoulders, and other negative body language must be kept in check.

You need to convey the appearance of being collegiate, warm, friendly, open to suggestions and not fixed in your views, able to take criticism without losing your cool.

If you are unsure whether you have any of these habits ask a colleague for feedback, or do what was suggested earlier and video yourself. Are you giving off any negative or dismissive signals?

Try to stand up straight as you speak and don't hunch over the lectern.

Beware

Try to avoid giving out negative signals. You may be nervous and wish you were somewhere else but don't let this show.

Cast your gaze over the whole audience as you speak. Try to look at the right side, then move to the middle, then to the left. It is difficult to do this, and you will favor one part of the audience but the side you neglect will feel they are not as involved.

Write it down!
Keep working at it and if need be write down on a card *"Remember to look at the audience!"* Keep this in front of you while you speak then when you glance down it will remind you to look at all parts of the audience. It's not rocket science but you would be amazed (or maybe you wouldn't) by how many lecturers either fail to look at the audience at all, or only ever look at one section.

You can, of course, pick out specific faces to smile at so long as one is from the right, the center and the left. From afar it will not be obvious to the audience members that you are staring at one person – each will feel you are looking at him or her.

Add a Dramatic Dimension

Pauses are useful

We have already discussed the uses of pauses during a speech. These add a heightened sense of drama and make the audience listen more keenly.

You can also use the time it takes for the information to sink in to pick up a glass of water and have a drink. This gives you time to reflect and lets the audience absorb what you have just said.

You can add drama by using specific types of slides such as slides with one word on them or slides with no words at all. The blank slide along with a real pause in your delivery will make your speech more dramatic.

You could always shout (in moderation!) For example, you might say *"80% of new businesses fail in the first 3 years. But it needn't be that way!"*

Avoid running around on the stage

Perhaps it's best to avoid the sweaty Steve Ballmer look when he gave a talk at a Microsoft convention some time ago. He was running around, shouting and perspiring heavily. Although, to his credit, this was definitely a *memorable* presentation!

Find your own methods of emphasis, using whatever feels comfortable for you without doing anything too zany or gimmicky.

Avoid dramatic slide effects or transitions

Lots of people I have seen presenting use built-in slide effects in PowerPoint and Keynote. These vary from the more subtle rotating cube in Keynote to text that flies onto the slide with a typewriter sound as each letter hits the screen. Initially, the audience may find this mildly amusing but after a while it becomes irritating. Avoid using software to create drama.

Alas, poor Yorick! I knew him...

Can you use amateur dramatics to liven things up? Why not? If you can create tension by using acting techniques then use them by all means.

Use *anything* to drive your message home!

End Your Talk Elegantly

Just as the beginning of a presentation is tricky and needs much practice, so too, does the end. You want the final couple of slides to be high impact. These slides will contain a summary of what you have said, and at the end of the speech they should contain the key messages that you want the audience to focus on and recall after the presentation is over.

Just as you have rehearsed the Introduction over and over again, do the same for the ending. You want the delivery to be crisp and clear. The key messages are the main (possibly the only) things you need them to remember from your talk.

The end is nigh

You need to recognize that you are coming to the end of your presentation and never be caught unawares *"Oh, I thought I had one or two more slides, but never mind...In conclusion..."*. The slide before your Conclusion slide must be known to you so that you can wrap up the "new" information you give to the audience. Then, when you advance you will see the Conclusion slide or whatever you want to call it (*Conclusion, Finally, Final Thoughts, Summary,* etc). Here you want to have only three or possibly four messages. You should distil the entire presentation into three or four points which must be made simply, rather than four densely packed paragraphs containing bullets and sub-bullets!

Hone your key point to perfection

Can you do this? It takes skill and very careful editing or you could look at the notes you made when you started writing your speech. Did you write down the key messages before you started writing? If you did, just use those as your concluding remarks.

Some people use a *"Thank You"* or *"Any Questions?"* slide but I don't think these add much. It is probably better to end with something like *"Thank you for listening. I would be happy to take any questions"* or *"Thank you for your attention"*. Then stand back a little from the podium while they applaud. You can leave your Conclusions slide in place or advance to a blank slide.

Don't forget

A graceful conclusion to your speech is just as important as a strong beginning. Practice the ending of your speech as much as the introduction.

127

International Audiences

Speaking internationally is a minefield. You will have an audience whose command of your language is variable. Some will understand every word and nuance while others will only have a basic grasp of the language.

- It is always advisable to slow your speech down whenever you are involved in public speaking. This is even more necessary when the audience is international

- If you fail to moderate your speech and your visuals you will lose some of the audience

- It is disrespectful to them to assume they will be able to understand your language and your accent. It's their problem. Actually, it's *your* problem. This is about them and you are supposed to be providing this speech for them

Achieve a good balance when speaking to an international group?

Firstly, you must accept that you must deliver your speech much more slowly than you would normally. If you usually use 20 or 25 slides then reduce this to about 15 for the international audience. You are going to have to speak more slowly, explain concepts more clearly, point out items on diagrams and figures more carefully. This all takes time and it will slow you down.

Avoid using abbreviations

As well as this, avoid using abbreviations that might be quite different in other languages. Try to use the full term for items such as "Intensive Care Unit" rather than "ICU".

If you deliver your speech in a more measured way than usual, and avoid abbreviations and explain your slides then the audience will be able to keep up with you and they will be much happier.

Be sensitive to cultural issues

The other aspect of international speaking to remember is the cultural one. Colors have different meaning in different cultures – red means happiness in China but anger in the West, whereas white signifies death in China. In certain cultures women must cover their head with a scarf. If you are meeting a group of businessmen in Japan there will be the exchange of business cards; accept their business cards with both hands, read front and back

Don't forget

Be sensitive to local cultural issues when talking at international meetings.

then place in a wallet. When handing yours to them do so with both hands with the text the right way up for them to read, they may bow to you and you should bow back. Ask the organizers what is expected culturally of you so that you minimize the risk of making a major *faux pas*.

It's best not to get too hung up on the dos and don'ts of international speaking but be aware of their needs and try to be considerate. Just imagine if you were listening to a talk in French and you only knew a little French. How would you want the speech delivered to you? Ask the organizers for any hints or tips they have about the culture, or check online.

Web resources

There are many websites dealing with international business customs. You can adapt this advice to suit your needs. Check out *http://www.executiveplanet.com* and *http://www.cyborlink.com*.

This site is Cross Country Navigator (*http://www.countrynavigator.com*) which provides a huge amount of information on travel, culture, and other useful information for all travelers, especially those involved in business.

Summary

- As we have said previously, giving a speech, a lecture, delivering a eulogy is a performance

- You should try to have poise and style

- Be larger than life but not totally outrageous

- You want them to remember you and your speech – at the very worst you want them to remember your key messages long after the show is over

- Although difficult, try to relax as much as possible but not too much. You do not want to be totally laid back – some adrenaline helps keep you sharp and focused. It will enhance your performance

- Audience engagement is critical. Look at them – not at the screen even if you are nervous. They want to feel involved

- Make sure you start your presentation strongly. This part is often the most nerve wracking. When you practice, concentrate on the first few opening sentences. Get these embedded in your head so that, even when a little anxious, you will appear confident and polished

- Write notes, annotate your handouts and take these to the lectern. Hopefully you will not need these, but the reassurance that they are there is a help to many speakers

- Be gracious and never arrogant, even if you *are* a big cheese

- Remember to thank the organizers for the kind invitation to speak

- Watch your body language. Avoid slouching, biting your nails, playing with coins in your pockets or with your hair. You want to stand upright, gazing at the entire audience throughout your speech

- Make your speech more memorable by adding dramatic elements – such as statistics, quotations, and other snippets that get the audience's interest

- Try to end your talk as smoothly as you started it. A simple *"Thank you for your attention"* is often sufficient

9 Taking Questions

Taking questions from the audience is one part of public speaking most people dread the most. Learn how to handle quiet audiences as well as the loud aggressive ones that throw brickbats at you!

Remain Calm!

The Question & Answer session is feared by the inexperienced presenter mainly because it is the one area which is outside your control. You don't know which questions you will be asked. The other big worry is that you won't know how to answer. Actually, you can control this to a certain extent, and we will discuss this later.

The Question section of any talk gives you a great opportunity to shine. You need to think on your feet and if you handle the questions well, you will look good.

It also provides a chance to add in some of the detail you had to leave out of the speech because of time constraints.

You need to remain calm. You have done the real hard work and you have almost finished. This is the final part so you do not want to blow it now.

After the applause has died down, take a drink of water while you wait for the questions to start. Take a few deep breaths and mentally calm yourself down.

Listen to the question carefully, and keep a pen and paper nearby so you can jot down any words the questioner has used just in case you are flustered and don't take it all in. Sometimes just jotting down the *key words* in the question can help.

It is a good idea to repeat the question back to the questioner so you can be sure you understood it correctly. If the questioner did not use a microphone the rest of the audience might not have heard the question so you are making sure they know what has been asked.

"OK, if I have understood this correctly, what he is asking is ... and ....". Repeating the question also gives you extra time to think.

Give yourself time

Give yourself enough time to think of your response and try to break down your answer into several points if you can. This can save you feeling flustered, or having to ask for the question to be repeated since you have forgotten what was asked. Pausing while you formulate your answer looks much more measured than if you were to launch straight into your answer even if you know exactly what the answer is.

Predicting Questions

Some questions are predictable
There are many questions that can be predicted well in advance of the speech. Maybe you have been to talks on a similar topic – can you recall any of the questions the speaker was asked?

Questions learned from experience
If you have given this, or a similar, talk before, what were you asked on those occasions? Did you write the questions down? Did you write answers alongside the questions? Try to keep a sheet containing all possible questions along with their model answers so you can give really slick answers if the questions come up again.

Spot the obvious questions
Look through your presentation once it is written, and see if you can spot anything that they might want elaborated. Methods? The How? Or Why? of what you are doing. In scientific talks the audience often want to know more of the detail about the methods used in the work. Or they may ask about additional experiments which you may have conducted or perhaps you are doing those now, but do not yet have the data to present here. They generally want to know about the downsides of treatments (side effects, costs), or products (competitors, patents, the real unmet needs, predicted forecasts in terms of sales and revenue), how will this way of working really change practice or behavior, and how are you going to measure this?

Plant questions for the audience to ask
As you present you can set up some "plants" such as "*Why does this happen? We're not quite sure but we have a few ideas. Maybe we could discuss this at the end if we have time*". Think of questions you would *hate* to be asked, then work out model answers for these.

Political questions
Sometimes knowing who will be in the audience will help you work out some of the questions. You may know the views of some audience members, and be aware that they have likes and dislikes, or they may have specific beliefs about certain things. If, in your speech, you are challenging these views you can expect questions on this part of the speech. Or you may be speaking to pharmacists about a new drug product. Their interest is in safety, cost and effectiveness so you need to have those answers ready since they will almost certainly ask questions in this area.

Questions During the Speech

During informal presentations to smaller groups (up to 20 or 30) it is more fun to take questions as you go along. Try to break the ice right at the beginning *"I am delighted to be able to talk to you today and we've got about one hour. Rather than me just lecturing for the whole time why not just shout out if anything I say doesn't make sense, or you think needs elaboration? Thanks."*

Quite often there may be points in the presentation that are not completely clear. If you take questions only at the end, the questioner might not feel like raising the question, or may worry that you answered the point later in the presentation but isn't sure. Stopping you as you go through the material makes sure they understand *now* and so any misconceptions can be cleared up early on so the rest of your presentation makes complete sense.

Hot tip

Questions taken during a presentation are useful since you can explain things as you go along rather than store everything up until the end of the speech.

Questions during the talk breaks the whole thing up, and stops the monologue. It also gives you time to catch your breath, have a quick drink of water and maybe have a think about where the presentation is going.

Try to involve the others. *"That's really interesting. I am not sure I agree 100% – what does anyone else think? Do you agree with him?"* Look for non-verbal cues such as people frowning, shaking their heads or perhaps people nodding in agreement. Throw open the floor and try to get the others involved.

Questions at the End

This is the norm for formal speeches. You stand up, talk for however long you have been allocated, then stop for questions.

Try to make sure your question time is not eroded by speaking too long. This commonly happens. Speakers have too many slides for the time slot and they use up their question time. If the audience start asking questions you will use up the time meant for the next speaker if there is one. Alternatively a very strict Chairman might insist on moving straight to the next speaker so there is no time for questions after your speech. The audience will be unhappy if this happens and they will mark you down as someone who is not organized and a bad timekeeper.

In this type of Question & Answer session, the questioner poses a question which you then answer as best you can. Either you or the chairman can select the next questioner.

Cast your net wide

If the audience is large, it is a good idea to choose questions from all parts of the room to make them feel you are including the whole audience and not just the chosen few who are sitting right down at the front. In fact, for all audiences try to spread the questions from as many sections as possible. Audiences do like to feel involved and engage with the speaker and this is one way of ensuring the whole group gets involved.

Thank the questioner

Don't go overboard here but do thank the questioner by using a variety of phrases such as *"You have raised an interesting point…"*, *"That's a good question…"*, *"Thanks for that. This is something that puzzled me for a while and…"*, *"That's a great question."* And so on.

Why is it important to thank them?

Because it is polite, and shows that you can listen as well as speak. It shows you are open to suggestions and you might even change your opinion based on what one of the audience says. Some great ideas have come from audiences asking questions!

It also shows that you have *humility*.

You've Lost Me...

What if you can't hear or understand the question?

Sometimes the acoustics are terrible and it's really difficult to hear what is being asked. Don't just bluff your way through – ask for the question to be repeated *"I'm sorry, I didn't catch all of that, can you just repeat it for me?"*

Once they repeat the question, repeat it back to the questioner so you can be sure you have understood what is being asked.

Sometimes the questioner hasn't used the microphone and you might need to ask him or her to wait for the microphone to reach them before repeating the question.

If you can hear it but don't understand it you will have to admit this *"Thanks. I'm not sure I fully understand what you are asking. Are you saying …?"*. They may nod in agreement in which case you can then answer. If they are shaking their head then you still haven't understood. Can you ask for it to be rephrased yet again? If there is a Chairman, maybe they will step in on your behalf and say *"We still don't understand what you are asking. Can you try rephrasing it again?"* This means less embarrassment for you since the third party has stepped in on your behalf.

Help! I cannot answer this question

Do you know everything about the subject? I doubt it. No-one knows the answer to everything so one day you will be asked a question to which you do not know the answer. You could pretend you know and make something up but this is never advisable. It is far better to say *"That's an interesting question but I am not sure I know the answer"* you can then talk about something related which might help the questioner *"What I can tell you, though, is…"*. This may help or it may not.

Be honest with yourself and the audience

Honesty is always the best policy. If you don't know, then simply admit that you don't know. It would be astonishing if you could answer every single question and it's sometimes good to look human. You can offer an opinion, however, and say something like *"I think … but I am not entirely sure, sorry."*

Maybe you could offer to get the questioner's details or email address after the session and get back to him?

Beware

If you cannot answer a question be honest and say so.

Hostile Questions

Before you start the Question & Answer session, ask people to identify themselves when they wish to ask a question. Ask them to state who they are and where they work. This will put some hostile people off since they won't want to be remembered.

This happens. Sometimes people have an axe to grind, or feel they know more than you. It can be disconcerting, especially if the whole show has gone smoothly up until then.

Don't take it personally

How can you tell it is hostile? Generally the person's tone will give it away, or other body language such as pointing at you, or jabbing the air, they may use provocative language.

Above all, remain calm and professional. It will not help your cause if you become aggressive too.

You are in charge so it is up to you to set the example. The audience will be firmly on your side.

Remain firm but be friendly. Maintain eye contact with the questioner. If you understand the question answer it in plain terms and then move on to the next question.

If they won't let it drop say something like "*Well, I think we'll have to agree to disagree on that one but maybe we could take another question*" (and point to someone else with their hand up).

Try to stick to the facts and if need be refer back to your speech. Don't get taken down the path of opinion since it will be difficult to reach agreement here.

Let's chat later

Sometimes just taking the conversation offline helps. If you have someone who clearly does not and will not agree with you, suggest you chat after the meeting, give them your business card and suggest they contact you and you can talk further.

Hot tip

Do your utmost to remain calm if you are questioned by a hostile member of the audience.

The Quiet Audience

Some audiences are quiet. You can give the same presentation to two groups containing the same number of people, all of much the same grade and one can be so lively you can hardly get through your content, and the other can be a wall of silence.

Have some planned questions of your own which you can throw out to the audience to see if they take the bait. "*I haven't used X very much, but some of you may have done so and may wish to share your experiences here*". Or you could elaborate on some of the points made during your speech to see if you can get them motivated. "*You will remember I mentioned X, earlier. We don't know why it failed and we are still trying to puzzle this out. Maybe someone in the audience has tried this?*"

It is well known that the worst time to give a speech or presentation is immediately after the lunch break, when the audience is likely to be listless, full and less responsive. Sometimes people fall asleep – which is not a problem as long as they don't snore.

It may be helpful to acknowledge that after working hard all morning, and having had a large lunch, it is likely they will have less energy in the Question & Answer sessions.

You may need to plan to involve and interact with the audience more after lunch by preparing a few controversial questions to ask them.

Try questions like:

- "*Has anyone tried...*"

- "*Do you think ... is useful?*"

- "*Where do you think this would work?*"

- "*Why does ... always fail?*"

- "*I can't see ... ever being of any benefit. Is there anyone who disagrees with me on this one?*"

- "*I think ... is a total waste of time and money and should be abandoned immediately*"

- "*Has anyone here used ... and is prepared to describe what it's like?*"

Don't forget

Not every audience is interactive. They may say little and ask few questions. You may have to work to encourage them.

Learning From Experience

The Question & Answer session will boost your confidence

Once you have closed the Question & Answer session and taken your seat in the audience you take a big sigh of relief. Well done! You have entertained and informed and now you have satisfied them with your answers.

Your confidence will be much greater. In fact you'd love to do the whole thing all over again! Your nerves have gone and you feel totally in control. Hold that thought, since you will need it for the next time you give a presentation.

Make notes from the questions asked

Jot down as many of the questions as you can remember. Note down the answers you gave so you can work on these and perfect them for the next time and appear even more slick.

What could be better?

Reflecting on the whole experience, is there anything you felt you could have done better? How would you improve it next time?

Was the opening strong? If not, why not? Make some notes about this and see if you can improve on it for the next time.

Was your pace right? Did you manage to fit the speech in to the allotted time? Maybe it was even shorter which is great. Or was it because you were speaking too fast?

There will be some negative aspects but don't dwell on these. Just make a note for next time so you can improve on it.

Seek feedback

You might want to ask any colleagues who were in the audience what they thought of your performance. Or you can ask to see the evaluation forms which delegates fill in during sessions at many conferences.

Summary

- As with the delivery of your speech, staying calm is critical during the Question & Answer session

- Many questions may be predicted. You may have given this talk before – think about what questions you were asked last time. Look at the content of your speech – what questions are they likely to ask? What questions would *you* ask if you heard this speech?

- Sometimes it can be useful to take questions as you go through your speech. There may be difficult concepts that are better explained at the time, rather than right at the end

- Conventionally, and especially with large audiences, questions are taken right at the end

- Sometimes you will not understand what is being asked. Simply ask for it to be repeated or rephrased

- Do you know everything? No, of course not. So, if you are asked a question to which you do not know the answer simply say so. We are only human

- Some questioners may be hostile and ask questions in a hostile manner. Their beef will probably not be with you but often they are simply seeking attention, or they are put out that they are not giving the talk

- Whatever the reason, you should be civil and collegiate in your response. Answer as best you can in a calm manner, then move on to the next question

- Some audiences are quiet and ask very few questions. You could simply stand down and move to the next speaker or you could try to get them involved by asking what they feel about specific aspects of the material

- Try to use the Question & Answer session as a means of further reinforcing your key messages

- Refer back to these when you give your answers

- Avoid bringing in new material during this part of the presentation. It can confuse the audience

10 Speaking Occasions

Public speaking takes many forms, from the informal family gathering, reciting eulogies at funerals and saying farewell to colleagues who are leaving your business. Professionally we need to be able to teach through lectures, sell our goods to others and persuade investors to lend us money. In this chapter, the aim is to provide background information for most of the common speaking events.

Best Man's Speech

Preparation time
Two to four weeks needed to collect background information about the bride and groom.

Potential anxiety rating
Moderate.

Dress
Formal, as directed by the Bride and Groom. Try not to drink too much alcohol before your speech (keep that till later!)

Formality
Formal.

Microphone use
Not generally required.

Use of script
Some people may use a script, but it would be better to use the index card method with headings on each one. Place all relevant details related to that heading on the card. For example note down funny anecdotes.

Try not to drone on for a long period. The guests will get bored and the humorous anecdotes will start to grate. Keep it short if you can (5–10 minutes).

Visual props
Not generally used.

Opening lines
Ask the audience for their attention. It is likely there will be a great deal of conversational buzz. Perhaps tap a glass with a spoon. You should thank the bride and groom for asking you to be the Best Man. You should also thank the parents of the bride and groom, and refer to them by name and make it clear which ones are the parents of either the bride or the groom. It is worth

mentioning how you met the couple and how long you have known them. Base the speech around one or two funny stories about the couple.

Keep your index cards with you and add little snippets but don't try to cram too much in. Avoid any scandalous stories or anything that reflects badly on either the bride or the groom. Keep rereading your speech and refine the content.

Copy the speech onto fresh cards ready for the big day.

Topics to include
Early life, university antics, holiday adventures.

Humor
Appropriate but keep it tempered i.e. avoid sexual innuendo, or otherwise hurtful jokes.

How to end
Your last card should prompt you to announce the toasts. Wish the couple well in their married life.

You might want to recite a poem (short) or deliver a one liner such as *"Here's to the bride - may she share everything with her husband...and that includes the housework"*, *"Here's to the groom, a man who kept his head even while he lost his heart"*, or *"Here's to the new husband, and here's to the new wife, may they remain lovers, for all of life."*

Make sure everyone has a drink ready (fill any empty glasses) and ask everyone to raise their glasses and say *"To Mary and Paul"* then the audience should say *"To Mary and Paul"*, raise their glasses and drink a toast to the bride and groom.

Birthdays

Preparation time
One or two days. This should be a very short speech (3-5 minutes at most).

Potential anxiety rating
Mild.

Dress
Casual.

Formality
Informal.

Microphone use
Not required.

Use of script
Not required.

Visual props
Not needed.

Opening lines
This should be a very positive upbeat speech. The content should be suitable for all age groups since there may be children or elderly family members attending.

Topics to include
Almost anything but avoid scandalous material or topics that reflect negatively on the person. Probably best not to mention the person's age unless it is a major milestone (e.g. 21 or 50 years old).

Humor
Works well in this type of celebratory speech.

How to end
You can end fairly simply, make a toast or even use a quote such as *"The most effective way to remember your wife's birthday is to forget once."*, *"I don't feel old. I don't feel anything till noon."* (Bob Hope), or *"A true friend remembers your birthday but not your age."*

Hot tip

If you want to remain friends it is sometimes wise not to mention how old the person is when you are speaking at their birthday party!

Leaving Parties

Preparation time
One week or less.

Potential anxiety rating
Mild.

Dress
No specific dress code.

Formality
Informal.

Microphone use
Not generally required.

Use of script
Not necessary.

Visual props
Not necessary.

Topics to include
You will want to let people know how you know the person, how long you have worked together and in what capacity. Tell them how long the person has worked at the company and highlight any landmarks, for example working his or her way up from being junior to senior partner. Has he or she had any major successes or achievements during the period they have worked there? If so, let the audience know about these. You might want to bring in one or two humorous anecdotes about the person. If the person is retiring, find out what their hobbies are and mention these and allude to the fact that he or she will be spending plenty of time in these pursuits rather than commuting to the office each day.

Humor
Works well in this setting.

How to end
Wish them well in their new post and ask them to keep in touch with people in the office. Hand over the gift if there has been a collection prior to the leaving party. The leaver should then say a few words of thanks. The leaver should have a few notes jotted down on a card or piece of paper and be ready to thank everyone for coming.

Don't forget

Do some research and find out some interesting facts about the person who is leaving.

Funerals and Eulogies

Preparation time
At least one week, two or more would be better.

Potential anxiety rating
Moderate to severe.

Dress
Formal, dark suit, black tie, white shirt.

Formality
Formal.

Microphone use
Not generally used.

Use of script
Can be used but try to make good notes, commit these to memory then recall the speech.

Visual props
Not appropriate.

Humor
Gentle humor may ease tension but use very carefully and sensitively.

Content
Writing and delivering a eulogy is an honor but is a difficult speech both to write and to deliver. Aim to create a speech of remembrance, capturing that person's life and achievements.

Talk to friends and family so you can build up a complete picture of the deceased's life. You are aiming to help the audience remember the deceased by painting a picture in words, covering his or her life, achievements and notable memories.

Mention the person's age, where they were born, their early life, school, college and career. Mention their partner and any children they have. If the deceased was a strong family person say so, and bring in any happy family anecdotes. Did they have any special interests or hobbies? Were there any notable achievements in his or her life? Outline these for the audience. Most people have achievements of some sort, so do mention these.

Don't forget

Eulogies, although sad, are also an opportunity to celebrate the life of the deceased.

How did you know the person? Note down early memories of activities that involved you both. Some may be humorous, so include these since it makes the story more personal.

By now you will have a fairly detailed picture of the person and you want to start putting this into some kind of order. You could use index cards and start noting things down chronologically. This will give you a framework for building the rest of the speech. Once you have the information on the cards try drafting the speech.

Once you have your first draft, refine the text. You might want to transfer the information to a word processor to make the editing easier. You could give each "section" a separate page if that helps break up the content.

Read through the whole speech a number of times. Try saying it out loud. Are the words used the sorts of words you would normally use in conversation? Use conversational English – this will make it sound natural, sincere and more touching.

You should not read verbatim but condense the speech into a series of headings. If you have practiced enough you will not need to see all the text below the headings.

This is the most emotional type of public speech you will have to deliver. Remember to introduce yourself so that the audience knows what your relationship was to the deceased.

You may be in complete turmoil and find it difficult to speak. Make sure you have tissues and water to hand. Try to be as relaxed as possible and take some deep breaths. Start slowly to build your confidence. If you find some pieces difficult to say, or you feel you may cry, pause for a second or two to compose yourself.

If you really feel you are too emotional to continue the speech ask someone to take over (if you feel beforehand that this might happen, have someone ready and primed to take over for you). This person should know the content of the eulogy.

How to end
Not critical. Perhaps give a final thought or two then bow your head and walk back to your seat but do what feels natural.

Business Meetings

Preparation time
One to two weeks depending on level of meeting (internal meeting may need little preparation whereas external meeting with major funders may require two weeks or more to plan).

There may be much at stake here, so plan well. Consider all eventualities and be prepared for a real grilling during the question session.

Potential anxiety rating
Mild to moderate.

Dress
Formal, business attire.

Formality
Varies depending on whether internal (semi-formal) or external (formal).

Microphone use
Not generally required.

Use of script
Not advisable.

Visual props
You may wish to use a flip chart or PowerPoint but let them know in advance if the latter so they can set up the necessary equipment, or bring your own laptop.

If you do decide you want to use slides remember they may not have a projector and you may have to use your laptop display to show the slides. Make the slides text-light with large fonts so they can all see the content of the slides.

If you are using a projector it will be much easier to see the slide content.

Opening lines

The whole pitch depends on the setting. You need to know the make-up of the audience, where they work, their roles, what they already know about you and your project.

Internal meetings

Internal meetings will need little introduction. If you are meeting with an external audience you will need to have a very crisp presentation with a clear opening (why you are there, what you represent and what you are seeking). There should be a body of information containing background development, information about prototypes, markets, opportunities, unmet needs. Finish with a clear statement of what you are asking from them. Why them? What can they offer? What is in it for them? Attention span in busy executives tends to be short so make the whole speech about 15 minutes leaving plenty of time for questions.

External meetings

What you say and how you conduct the meeting depends very much on the situation, whether you are there to sell, persuade, or perhaps this is an advisory board meeting where you are seeking advice from outside experts.

Topics to include

Those relevant to the pitch. Try to stay focused.

Humor

May be used but not usually needed in this style of speech.

How to end

With a clear statement of what you are seeking. Thank them for listening and leave plenty of time for questions. Answer questions succinctly and honestly. If you don't know an answer tell them you will get back to them later.

Beware

Stay sharp and focused during business meetings if you want to impress. Time is money to these guys, so a punchy, direct presentation is preferred.

Roundtables & Advisory Boards

Preparation time
One week or less.

Usually you will be sent information to read ahead of the meeting. You may also receive a printed slide deck and background information about the company. You will also be given a Confidentiality Agreement form to sign.

Your role is to provide advice to the company, helping identify any pitfalls in their plans, and helping to shape their strategy. The conversation will include all advisers along with a number of company representatives. You will speak either when asked a

direct question or if you have something specific to say about the points being discussed. These are often chatty affairs, though it is likely someone will either be recording the whole "conversation" or making extensive notes as people speak.

Potential anxiety rating
Mild to moderate.

Dress
There is no dress code for this type of meeting. Usually smaller companies will try to impress by dressing very smartly, but since you are there as an adviser, you can wear an open neck shirt, chinos, or suit with no tie. Smart casual would do fine.

Formality
Semi formal. It is likely that you will know some of the attendees, especially if there are several experts present, of which you will be one. You may also know some of the company people and this will help with maintaining a relaxed feel. But make no mistake, these meetings are expensive to run and they have asked you there for business reasons. This is *not* a social event!

Microphone use
If there are many people attending there may be microphones on the table (tables are often placed in a horseshoe shape with the advisers around the "U").

Sometimes the company may ask permission from the advisers to record the meeting (audio only).

Use of script
Not needed.

Visual props
None, unless you are planning to give a short presentation during the meeting, which sometimes happens. In this case you will be asked in advance to prepare something. If you are running the advisory board then you will probably wish to present data, research, proposals and other information to the advisers. More than likely you will use a PowerPoint template specifically designed for the company, with the logo fixed, and colors preset. Try to ensure your slides are easy on the eye with limited detail.

Opening lines
Not needed.

Topics to include
This is guided by the agenda for the meeting.

Humor
Not generally used.

How to end
This is not a formal speech so you do not need to make the concluding remarks. This will be done by the company who has requested the meeting.

Unexpected Speeches

Preparation time

None, though you should note down some headings on an index card or two and keep it with you, or use a PDA, mobile phone or other light portable device to keep some notes about major ongoing projects so you can discuss if called upon.

At work, you are most likely to be asked something relating to your current projects. You should know these fairly well, anyway, and not need to think too hard before giving an answer.

If you are really stuck think *past*, *present* and *future*: we used to do things this way, it was a problem so we changed to something else which we are doing now, but our big plan is to do something completely different.

If it is a topic which is completely out of the blue then obviously you cannot plan for this. Instead use the skills you have learned: take a deep breath, break it down into some big headings (in your head) then speak slowly. Other points will come to mind once you start speaking.

Occasions where unexpected speeches take place

- During a celebratory dinner
- At a retirement or leaving party
- After the launch of a product
- When you are successful in bidding for a grant, or other money
- Birthdays, weddings, and other family events
- At ceremonies, prizegivings, dances or balls

Hot tip

Impromptu speeches can (to an extent) be prepared in advance. If you think there's a chance you may be asked to talk, do your homework and have something ready!

- During business meetings

- After any event which has a major impact on your business or family

Potential anxiety rating
You may be *surprised* to be asked but since there is no warning you will not be stressed ahead of the event.

Dress
No specific requirement.

Formality
Varies.

Microphone use
You may need to use a microphone if the group is big and there's already a microphone in use at the meeting or event. Often you will just have to speak loudly since there will be no microphone but since this should be a fairly short and sweet speech it should not matter.

Use of script
Not required.

Visual props
None needed, but you might want to grab a flip chart if you want to use this to help explain your ideas.

Opening lines
"Thanks for the opportunity to talk about this project. As you know we have been working hard on this since…" or *"Sure, I'd be delighted to tell you a bit about this. Basically…"*

Topics to include
Those relevant to the question being asked.

Humor
This would be useful in an informal discussion or meeting, but probably not at a press conference.

How to end
Say something like *"So that's where we are. I'd be happy to take questions, but if not, I'll hand you back to John. Thanks."*

Job Interviews

Preparation time
Two to four weeks.

Potential anxiety rating
Moderate to severe anxiety.

Dress
Smart.

Formality
Generally formal unless it is "trial by sherry" where you have drinks with people from the company and are asked a number of questions, hoping you might open up more than if sitting across a desk.

Microphone use
Not required.

Use of script
Not advisable.

Visual props
None needed unless they ask you to give a short presentation before the interview (once popular, but less so now).

Opening lines
None.

Topics to include
Those relevant to the discussion. Be guided by the interviewers. They will ask specific questions. Answer in a calm manner. Try not to say too much or lead yourself into areas where you would rather not go in case they start probing. When asked a question by an interview panel member, look at that person but also look at the others, much as you would do if you were giving a speech.

Humor
Not advisable.

How to end
The interviewers will normally ask if you have any questions. Do not ask about pay or benefits! Ask about their future plans, or internal courses, or opportunities for career development. Keep the questions simple so they can give a fairly brief answer.

Formal Lectures

Preparation time
One to two weeks.

Potential anxiety rating
Moderate.

Dress
Smart casual.

Formality
Fairly formal if there is a large audience.

Microphone use
Depends on the size of the audience. University lectures generally require use of podium or lapel microphone. Smaller tutorials would not require any amplification.

Use of script
Avoid.

Visual props
PowerPoint generally used, but if you can take your own laptop you might want to use Keynote, OpenOffice, NeoOffice, or other program.

Opening lines
For a student lecture you might say: "*Good morning/afternoon. I am John Doe one of the lecturers from the physics department and this session covers…*". If you are lecturing to a peer group at a conference say something like: "*Many thanks for that kind introduction. My name is John Doe and I am one of the senior physicists at X. I have been asked to discuss X today. So I will talk for about 20 minutes and then take questions.*"

Topics to include
Those relevant to the title of the lecture.

Humor
Some humor is often useful in formal lectures. It helps relax the audience and can be useful if the topic is fairly content-heavy.

How to end
"*Thank you for your attention. I would be happy to answer any questions/take questions from the floor*".

Hot tip

If you are giving a lecture, have the learning points clearly stated at the beginning. This provides the audience with a clear idea what will be covered during the lecture.

Informal Lectures

Preparation time
One to two weeks.

Potential anxiety rating
Mild to moderate.

Dress
Casual or smart casual.

Formality
Informal.

Microphone use
May be useful if the audience is large.

Use of script
Best avoided.

Visual props
You could use black/white board, flip chart or PowerPoint.

Opening lines
As for formal lecture although you can use a more casual tone. "*I am very pleased to be here today. I have been asked to talk to you about nuclear physics. I'd like to take the time to chat to you about…*"

Topics to include
Similar to a formal lecture but the style may be more interactive. You might want to use fewer visuals so you can spend time discussing points as they arise. Try to involve the entire audience.

Try to provoke questions and answers by throwing out suggestions like "*Are you all pretty much in agreement with what I just said? Looks like you are but I suspect one or two of you might feel differently.*" "*So what do you think of that. Does it sound reasonable?*"

Humor
This works in this setting but don't overdo it.

How to end:
Wrap up as you would with any lecture, go through your conclusion slide, stressing the key points that you have raised in the lecture. Thank them for their attention then take any further questions.

Group Discussions or Tutorials

Preparation time
One week.

Potential anxiety rating
Mild.

Dress
Casual.

Formality
Informal.

Microphone use
Not required.

Use of script
Not required.

Visual props
Flip chart may be useful.

Opening lines
No fixed introduction but as the leader of the tutorial group
you should introduce yourself, letting the tutees know which
department you are from and your role.

Tell them about the tutorial course and the expectations of them
(generally they prepare in advance and are given specific topics to
revise. This is then explored within the tutorial setting with your
role being moderator but with educational input).

Allow them to ask questions throughout the session, making the
event more conversational. They are there to learn and it is best to
eliminate any misconceptions early on.

Topics to include
As per the course.

Humor
Works in this setting but depends on the group and the topic.

How to end
Summarize what has been discussed, let them know the date,
time and location of the next tutorial and tell them what work is
required.

Keynote and Plenary Speeches

Occasion

These are formal invited talks but, unlike other speeches at a conference, they are reserved for the very best speakers or submitted abstracts. For a scientific conference the abstract committee review all the submitted abstracts, award these marks for scientific content and presentation. The top few are chosen to give *plenary* talks. This is the highest honor at

any conference and generally the audience attendance is high. The presenting author may not be the most experienced public speaker. In fact, it is likely that the person presenting is a junior member of the team.

In contrast, a *keynote* speech is usually a single talk presented by someone who is a major expert in his or her field. It is usual to dedicate a slot specifically for this one talk, which may last 45–60 minutes. Depending on the organization of the meeting the lecture may be didactic with no Question & Answer session.

Preparation time

Four weeks or more.

For these events you want your slides to be of the highest quality. More than ever, you want to be sure there are no typos, the graphics are good, the font size is sufficiently large and the slides are as uncluttered as possible. Ideally you should design your slide deck from scratch – don't recycle an old one.

Potential anxiety rating

Moderate to high.

Dress

Formal.

Beware

Keynotes and plenaries are big deals. Prepare these speeches down to the last detail.

Formality
Formal.

Microphone use
A microphone will be required. The event may be recorded as an audiovisual presentation. Organizations often use these by putting them online so people who missed the live event can watch them later. Sometimes they are burned onto DVD for the same purpose.

Use of script
Best avoided but you must know the content very well.

Visual props
Generally PowerPoint is used.

Opening lines: for a plenary talk
"Mr Chairman, I am very grateful to the committee for inviting me to give this plenary talk entitled X. I am a postdoctoral fellow in the John Doe lab and I will be presenting the results of my work into X. On the first slide…" or a variation thereof. Because of the formality of the occasion this type of talk follows a very standard format. There is little room for improvisation. You must design your slides carefully, and ensure you practice the speech many times, alone and in front of the research group or other members of the team. This helps you to iron out any weak parts of the presentation.

Topics to include
This is generally focused on a specific topic with little room to discuss other issues. Timing is very strict for plenary presentations e.g. ten minutes for the presentation with five minutes for questions. For the plenary there is usually no other speaker after your talk and you will be allowed slightly more than your allotted time if necessary.

Humor
This would not be advisable during a plenary talk but could be used in a keynote speech.

How to end
For the plenary use the standard *"Thank you for your attention"*. The keynote can be concluded depending on your style. You could just say *"Thank you"* or you could use *"Thank you for your attention"*.

Chairing a Small Meeting

This is a key skill and one that is often underestimated. A good chair can ensure a meeting goes smoothly and to time, with a consensus reached. A bad chair will have the opposite result.

One of the main roles of the chair is to be an impartial facilitator, ensuring the meeting achieves its intended aims. You should follow the agenda, make sure everyone is heard, and keep the meeting to time.

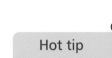

Hot tip

If you want to be a good chair, be impartial, considerate and try to provide balance during the meeting.

A good chair should:

Organize in advance, have a good working knowledge of the topics on the agenda, have a clear written agenda sent out well in advance, along with any relevant papers, know the committee members, be assertive but not domineering.

He/she must be able to stand his or her ground, keep everything on track, and summarize the meeting points – use this to wind up topics. Give everyone an overview of what was discussed and the action points agreed.

Be tactful

Work closely with the meeting secretary to agree the agenda and review the minutes of the meeting.

Finish on time

When running the meeting, the chair should introduce himself/herself, welcome new members, go round the table inviting the members to introduce themselves if there are new members present. The chair can use slides, overheads or flip charts as necessary. Invite outside speakers to present for specific items.

The chair should avoid dominating the meeting, talking too much, trying to cover too much detail, overrunning, taking sides in arguments, and forcing his or her ideas on the group.

How to Chair a Conference

This is a tough role, and is much more difficult than it looks. Acting as chair is more stressful than giving a presentation! You need to help plan the program, introduce the speakers, get the audience excited about the content, keep the speakers to time, and help with the Q & A session.

Program planning
Contact your speakers before the meeting and discuss titles for their presentations, and help them plan the content of their talks.

Research the speakers
You will need to introduce them to the audience so find out something about each speaker. Ask them to provide biosketches, and check their company or university website for information. If they are widely published, find out what their major contributions have been. Build them up, but try not to go overboard.

Warm up the crowd
You will need to open the meeting, thanking all the attendees for coming. Provide an overview of the meeting. Get them excited about the talks they are about to hear. Develop the theme of the session in order to put the speakers' presentations in context.

Introductions
Introduce each speaker using notes you have made. Write down key points on index cards, one for each speaker. Provide a glimpse of what the speaker will be discussing. Avoid reading your notes and make your style as conversational as possible. Invite the speaker onto the stage and begin the applause (the audience will follow your lead).

Keep speakers to time
When the speaker has used up the allotted time, you could move towards the podium, perhaps sitting at the desk on the stage. This alerts the speaker that his or her time has been used up.

Question session
Your role is to invite questions, asking the audience to use the microphones provided, stating their names and affiliation. You may wish to repeat questions so the speaker fully understands.

Finally
Thank all the speakers and thank the audience for attending.

Larger Audiences

This is most people's worst nightmare, and the sort of occasion which wakes us up at night in a cold sweat! Major conferences, expos, and the like often have a thousand or more delegates in the audience. Presenting confidently to this type of group takes practice, skill and technique.

You must prepare well in advance for this type of talk. You do not want to "wing it" in front of such a large group.

The pressure is high so you need to give it your best shot.

Put your speech together as you normally would for any speech but pay particular attention to the accuracy of your information, make sure you have the most up-to-date facts and a very clear idea of why you have been asked to speak.

- Write down your key messages and be sure in your own mind what you want to convey to this group. All work must now focus on these key points

- Use paper, index cards or whatever method you are comfortable with to generate the content

- Transfer to a computer, perhaps a word processor or slide program

- Sort the headings out first (with about one slide per minute but this may vary depending on your presentation style) then add the supporting text

- Once you are happy with this, you should obtain good quality images to add impact to your slide show. Try to make the images large and keep text to a minimum

- Avoid garish backgrounds. Keep the whole visual look as simple but as clear as possible

- Go over the content and practice extensively before the actual presentation. Say the speech out loud and present to one or two colleagues to make sure your meaning is clear

- Listen to any criticisms they may have and modify your slides accordingly

- Ensure you can deliver the speech in the time allowed – if you are unsure, cut back on material. Finishing early is acceptable. Overrunning is not

- Plan for questions. Predict as many as you can and ask the advice of colleagues in terms of what they think might come up. Write down your model answers and try to memorize these. This will make the Question & Answer session less stressful

- Speak slowly and deliberately. Watch the microphone – try to keep facing it so your volume does not vary

- Make eye contact with as many of the audience as possible as you speak to keep them involved

- Vary the pitch and speed of your delivery

- Use pauses where appropriate to stimulate thought and introduce tension

- When you have concluded, thank the audience for listening then stand back from the podium. They will then applaud

This may all seem very daunting at first and it does take practice and experience. An inexperienced public speaker should present to small audiences first then build up gradually. This helps build confidence. It is unfair to expect those with little exposure to large audiences to handle this situation well since anxiety levels will be extremely high.

International Audiences

The commonest setting is probably the international specialist conference. Many organizations in science, medicine and the business world host meetings abroad.

You may be invited to give a state-of-the-art lecture or perhaps a free communication. Either way, the advice is the same.

English is usually the preferred language. Most papers and communications are written in English.

Preparation

You need to prepare your presentation as you would for any presentation with a clear structure and memorable key points. Find out how long the talk is expected to last and how many minutes you will have for questions. Your speed of delivery will need to be considerably slower than for a native English-speaking audience. Use less slides to avoid the risk of overrunning your slot.

Delivery

Speak slowly and try to pause frequently to make sure the audience has taken in what you have just said. Don't rush from slide to slide since you will lose them early on and they may never catch up.

Remember

- Be aware of local culture e.g. clothing requirements for women (Islamic and some other Asian cultures)

- If you are meeting businessmen make sure you know how to greet them, and shake hands

- In Japan and some other countries you may have to bow – ask the person organizing the meeting how this is done

- In business, the exchange of business cards is expected. In the West, we tend to simply hand these out to people who often put them in their top jacket pocket with hardly a glance. In many cultures (especially Japan) you will be handed a business card face up, using both hands to pass the card. You are expected to read both sides of the card carefully before placing it in your own business card holder. Check out the web for advice concerning local culture and customs – for example *www.cyborlink.com*

- Don't overuse jargon, colloquialisms or talk too quickly or you risk losing an international audience

- Be aware of colors and their use in presentations. White is great for the US or Europe since it is associated with simplicity or purity but in Asian cultures it is associated with death. Red in China means happiness but in Western cultures it is often used for anger! Use something neutral

- If you are invited to eat a meal with your colleagues in that country you must try your best to eat, otherwise this will be taken as a signal of rejection

- Watch your body language – especially since many gestures and stances may be construed as threatening or impolite

- Research the culture of the country you are visiting. The Internet is a useful place to start

Do not

- Use colloquialisms and abbreviations – these will be largely meaningless in that culture

- Use acronyms – always say the full name

- Use political or other humor that may offend. Something which might seem funny to you may be deeply offensive to them

- Use humor – it often fails with English-speaking audiences so is not going to work where English is not the first language

- Use prolonged eye contact especially when close up – in many Asian and Islamic cultures this is seen as rudeness

- Use graphics that might offend. For example, a thumbs up photo would be associated as "well done!" or "good job!" in the US or Europe but it does not mean the same in all cultures

- Dress inappropriately – for men it is best to wear a suit and tie. For woman it might be advisable to wear a head scarf and cover the arms

Telephone Presentations

Presenting in a telephone conference is a form of virtual presentation. These are popular in business but less so in academia and education. It allows people in various locations to "get together" without actually being in the same room. Telephone conferences can also be used to present data, for example, in PowerPoint or other programs.

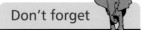

Don't forget

Before your telephone conference starts, have everything to hand because once proceedings begin it may be difficult to leave the room.

Preparation time
Variable, one week or less.

Potential anxiety rating
Mild.

Dress
Any.

Formality
Informal.

Microphone use
Not appropriate.

Use of script
May be used.

Visual props
Slides may be shown.

Opening lines
The leader should introduce himself or herself and thank everyone for joining the conference.

Topics to include
Those relevant to the discussion.

Humor
Not usually needed.

One person has to organize the telecon and is the leader. This person will have a leader "PIN" – a number which he or she has to enter after dialling the conference hosting company telephone number. Others will dial in at the same time and enter the predefined "Conference Code" which allows access to the telecon.

- The leader should introduce himself or herself and thank everyone for joining the conference

- The others should state their names and say who they represent

- An agenda needs to be prepared in advance and sent to the participants, with timings shown

- Supporting documents should be sent ahead of the meeting, allowing the participants time to read the content

- If you have PowerPoint slides you wish to go through, send these before the meeting. When the telephone conference starts ask people to open the PowerPoint document

- When taking people through a PowerPoint presentation use numbered slides. Say "*I am now moving to the next slide which should be Slide 7*", or whatever slide you are viewing

- If you are presenting – slow down and leave pauses after each sentence if possible. This also allows time for people to ask questions before you move to the next slide

- All participants may speak but only one at a time – it is very difficult to follow what is being said if two people try to talk

- Speech needs to be very clear and slower than usual since the participants cannot see each other

- Invest in a headset for your phone. Many of these have background noise canceling options

- At the end of the telecon wrap up the meeting, ask if there are any final points and thank everyone for attending

- The leader should make a list of off-line actions, such as emailing other documents to the group, calling people back at a later time so they can chat one-on-one about specific items

- The leader should also arrange the next telecon with the group if there is to be a follow-up conference

How to end

Thank the participants and arrange the date and time of the next telecon if appropriate. If there are papers to send out make sure it is clear whose job this is.

Webcasts

Preparation time
One or two weeks to prepare the slides.

Potential anxiety rating
Mild to moderate.

Dress
Business attire is probably best.

Formality
Presented formally.

Microphone use
Recording microphone is required.

Use of script
May be scripted to ensure all material covered in the correct order fitting the appropriate slides.

Visual props
PowerPoint most commonly used, but various web-based slide projection programs are available.

Opening lines
Introduce yourself and the topic. You may wish to provide a contact number, email address or URL in case people want to raise any points after the presentation is over. Alternatively questions may be taken live after the presentation.

Topics to include
Those relevant to the topic.

Humor
Not generally advised.

As the name suggests these are Internet-based broadcasts that can be given in real-time, or can be recorded in advance. They are fairly cheap to make and are popular in business, education, the media and music industry.

The technology involves creating an audiovisual presentation which is streamed to the viewer's computer. It does not have to be downloaded and watched later. In fact, streaming the content means that nothing has to be downloaded to the audience's computer.

Webcasts can be viewed by participants using their own PC or several people can get together in one room.

As a presenter this can be quite a stressful experience, since a live webcast has to begin at the allotted time, and once you start you cannot stop! So get everything ready before you start.

- Make sure you have some water near you in case your mouth dries up

- You will most likely be at your desk in front of a PC with the webcast software running. You will see your slides in a panel, and there will be other panels containing the participants' names, and other information

- Whether live or recorded, you will need a set of slides if you are giving a PowerPoint style presentation

- Make sure the slide content is crystal clear and you have not cluttered the slides with unnecessary detail

- Make yourself notes and have these in front of you

- Use index cards numbered the same as the slides. You should avoid reading these but since the audience will not see you, it is permissible to look through the content of the cards as you proceed through the presentation

- Speak slowly! Even more slowly than you would normally use for a presentation

- Introduce *pronounced pauses* between slides so that the listeners know you have finished with that slide and are about to move onto the next

- If possible, try to have a colleague nearby, listening. Ask someone who knows the topic well so that if you are asked any difficult questions they can help, or if you dry up during the speech itself they can help prompt you

How to end
Thank the audience for watching and give them the links if you wish people to contact you after the webcast.

TV and Radio Interviews

Preparation time
One or two weeks.

Potential anxiety rating
Moderate to high.

Dress
Smart business attire.

Formality
Formal (less so for radio).

Microphone use
Lapel microphones for TV, microphone on stand used for radio.

Use of script
Not advisable. Know your material well, have two or three key messages and retain these in your mind so you can get these messages across during the interview. Small soundbites are the norm.

Visual props
Not generally used.

Opening lines
Thank the host for inviting you to speak. Often there may be little time for pleasantries since they will want to move to the questioning fairly quickly.

Topics to include
Know your key messages well. Keep your answers aligned to the key messages and use bridges to get you back by saying things like "*So what this means is ...*" and bring in a key message. This helps you deal with the "*So what?*" question. Keep the answers simple and short. Do not say anything too vague or anything which might lead you down areas which you do not want explored, especially if the interview is live. If you are doing a recorded interview you can ask for specific aspects to be edited out.

Humor
Not generally used.

How to end
Thank the interviewer for the opportunity to share your information with the listeners or viewers.

Telephone Interviews

Preparation time:
One to two weeks.

Potential anxiety rating
Mild.

Dress, microphone use, visual prompts
Not relevant.

Formality
Informal.

Use of script
A sheet with key points to discuss will be useful.

Most of the initial talk will be done by the interviewer. Thank the person for inviting you to be interviewed. Ask who the interviewer is and who they represent. They may give you the questions in advance but often they do not. Make handwritten notes of key facts and figures in case these are asked during the interview.

Ask how long it will last before you agree to be interviewed. Ask whether this is live or just a means of collecting your responses. Visit the restroom in advance and have some water to hand in case your mouth dries up.

When asked questions, pause for a few seconds to make sure you have fully understood what is being asked and scribble down some notes as the interviewer speaks. Give your answer as a short clear response then await further questions. If they want more information they will ask for this. Refer to your notes if necessary and if you have PowerPoint slides on the topic you might want to have these open on your PC to refer to. If you have any papers (Word or otherwise) print these off and have them to hand in case you need to refer to them for specifics (costings, projections, results from experiments, and other information). If you do not know the answer to a question you must say so, and not make something up. There is no award for perfect answers or the highest score.

How to end
They will generally thank you, and ask if you have any questions.

Summary

- There are many occasions where public speaking is required

- Some are professional and others are personal

- Common to all of these is the need to know the rules of engagement – who the audience is, what they want to hear, and how best to pitch the speech itself

- Family events such as wedding, parties, and funerals are less demanding in the sense you have a "friendly" audience. You still need to plan your speech and rehearse but you do not have to be as polished as you would for a plenary talk

- Do your research well, and find out all you can about the people being discussed during this type of speech

- Avoid using anything inflammatory or embarrassing

- Social speeches can be factual, humorous and overall should be easy to listen to. Most social and family speeches are for entertainment, apart from one or two, for example the eulogy

- Eulogies are more serious speeches celebrating the life of someone who has recently died. But it is still permissible to use some humor during this otherwise serious speech

- Presenting at business meetings and advisory boards should be fairly slick. Keep your speech short and succinct leaving plenty of time for questions

- Education lectures whether formal or informal should have very clear learning objectives. These are analogous to the key messages used in business speeches. For the sake of the students, make sure the objectives are clear

- Keynotes and plenaries take much preparation – often weeks before the events themselves. Do not cut corners with speeches of this importance

- Handling large audiences is tricky for the novice speaker. It is better to gain confidence with smaller groups before moving on to the major meetings

- Be very aware of local cultural issues when you are presenting at international events

11 Further Resources

There are many resources to help us perfect our public speaking techniques, including books, websites and courses.

Books

Giving Great Presentations in Easy Steps, Drew Provan (In Easy Steps, 2009). This is the companion volume to Public Speaking in Easy Steps. It deals with the construction of presentations of varying types, provides tips on gathering your information and sorting this out into an orderly resource, helps you put together visuals to accompany your speech, teaches you how to use computers, flip charts, blackboards and other media to get your message across. The material in this book complements *Public Speaking in Easy Steps.*

How to Develop Self-Confidence and Influence People by Public Speaking by Dale Carnegie. This author was a great communicator. He is probably best known for his iconic work *How To Win Friends & Influence People* first published in 1936. The book has been revised and is published by Pocket Books.

In *How to Develop Self-Confidence and Influence People* he explores self-confidence showing how this can be developed. There are sections devoted to speaking clearly, how to prepare presentations, how to gain the audience's interest, and how to open and close your presentation. Dale Carnegie founded the Carnegie Institute, and there are communication training centers worldwide.

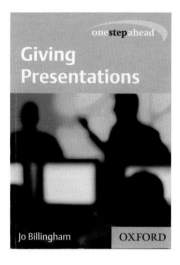

Giving Presentations, Jo Billingham (Oxford 2003) is a no-nonsense guide to planning and delivering a presentation, how to choose visual aids, and learn to present with confidence. Each section is short and is easy to read. There are hints

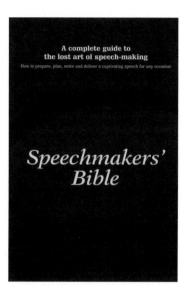

and tips down the right and left hand columns.

Speechmakers' Bible (anonymous, Cassell Illustrated) is a fairly large tome which includes pretty much what you would expect such as hints about preparing your speech, how to calm nerves, etc. There is also a section containing one liners to liven up the after-dinner speech.

Stand and Deliver. The Dale Carnegie Method to Public Speaking (Nightingale & Conant, 2008). This 5-CD set helps you identify

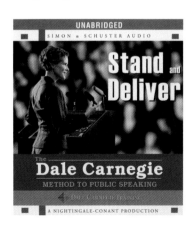

your authentic self so that you project an original style, gives you strategies to help you to win over any audience in one minute, as well as teaching you strategies that will ensure your listeners not only remember what you say, but make immediate and positive changes based on it. Finally, the program helps you deal with hostile questions. As a 5-CD set this takes a while to complete.

Courses

There are many courses run worldwide to help people overcome their fear of public speaking. For those with some experience there are courses that are designed to take your abilities to the next level, focusing on what you already know.

You may find that your institution runs courses of its own, and these are likely to be much cheaper than external courses. Try an internal course first and if you are still struggling or need help with specific areas attend an external course.

I have not provided details of the courses here because they all share common features such as overcoming anxiety, building confidence, engaging with the audience, keeping the audience focused on your presentation, handling Q&A.

www.CollegeOfPublicSpeaking.co.uk

This company runs courses throughout the year. In addition, there are online resources, newsletters, and famous speeches for downloading.

They also provide very useful hints and tips for people wishing to use PowerPoint, with training that helps you create presentations that do not simply contain the entire speech. Importantly, they cater for novices to people with some experience of presenting.

www.PublicSpeakingPro.co.uk

www.dalecarnegie.com

The name says it all here. World-renowned for training in communication this is arguably the gold standard in terms of professional coaching when it comes to public speaking.

Websites

TED (http://www.ted.com)

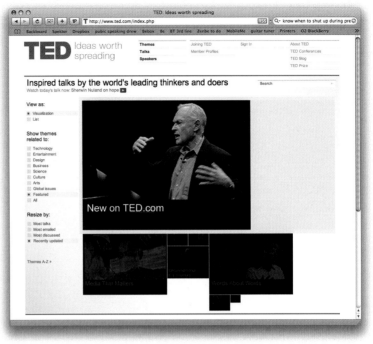

TED stands for Technology, Entertainment, Design. There is an annual conference attended by around one thousand participants. The material covered includes science, the arts and design, so there will be something for everyone.

The conference features speeches and presentations by inspiring presenters such as Seth Godin, Tony Robbins and Ken Robinson. The conference is sold out well in advance and is prohibitively expensive. However, free of charge, they make the best talks available to watch online.

If you are looking for ways to pep up your own presentation style you would learn much from watching these pros in action! Check out the website and watch the movies or download the audio or video podcasts from the iTunes store.

Toastmasters (http://www.toastmasters.org/)

This international non-profit organization hosts meetings in 92 countries worldwide. There are no instructors, and the meetings are run by the members. The aim is to improve presentation skills and communication techniques.

Meetings are held on a weekly basis and often use informal venues such as bars or public houses.

Other sites

- *http://connect.educause.edu/Library/Abstract/ EffectiveTeachingwithPowe/43763*

- *http://www.presentersuniversity.com/*

- *http://www.impactfactory.com/gate/public_speaking_training_ course/freegate_1552-1104-88327.html#fear*

- *http://www.sethgodin.com/sg/speaking.asp*

- *http://www.slideshare.net/Toastmasters*

- *http://www.premier-presentation.co.uk/TIPS.htm*

Quotations

If you intend to use quotations in your speeches (and sometimes these can work well if you choose appropriate quotations) then either get yourself a book of quotations (*Oxford Dictionary of Quotations* or *Concise Oxford Dictionary of Quotations*, Oxford University Press) or visit one of the websites offering free quotations.

Useful quotation sites

- *http://www.quotationspage.com*

- *http://www.quoteland.com*

- *http://www.bartleby.com/quotation*

- *http://www.theotherpages.org/quote.html*

- *http://www.brainyquote.com*

- *http://www.woopidoo.com/business_quotes*

- *http://www.brainybetty.com/bizquotes.htm*

- *http://www.saidwhat.co.uk/quotes/business/*

Finding Images For Slides

If you are going to add images to your slides try to use good quality graphics. Your company may have its own set of artwork for use in presentations so check in-house first.

There are sites offering free artwork but in general the quality is often poor. The software packages (PowerPoint, Keynote) themselves often contain clip art libraries which may feature some useful artwork but again, the quality is variable and worth avoiding.

Numerous sites will sell you royalty-free images which are usually very high quality photographs or vector graphics. You can pay per graphic or subscribe for a month or six months. Sites worth visiting include:

Shutterstock (www.shutterstock.com)

Both shutterstock, iStockphoto and Getty Images have tons of images (photos, vectors, line art, and clip art) for download. You can pay per image or subscribe for a month or longer. These are fairly expensive ways to get images but the quality is very high.

iStockphoto (www.istockphoto.com)

Getty Images (GettyImages.com/Royalty-Free)

Slide Sharing Sites

Rather than write a speech from scratch why not browse the slide sharing sites and see if there are any talks similar to the one you are going to give? There may be some text you could borrow or maybe the presentations will give you some inspiration needed to write your own talk.

Obviously it would be wrong to plagiarize these slides and pass them off as your own, but they are very useful for giving you design ideas. Seeing how other people use fonts, images and other aspects of design can help with the design of your own slides.

If you put together a slide presentation of which you are proud, you can upload these to slideshare and let others see your work.

www.slideshare.net is probably the best known site. There are talks on every conceivable topic, sometimes with video. Some authors will allow you to download their presentation but others will only allow viewing online with no download option. There is some great material here and some very talented communicators.

Another site is *www.authorstream.com* which also allows uploading and downloading of content.

The idea behind it is pretty much the same as slideshare but it's still worth browsing both sites to see if there are presentations of interest to you. There are even sites which feature specific areas, such as pathology (*www.aperio.com*).

Do a Google search for any topic you are interested in and include "slide share" or "image share" in the search criteria. You will be amazed at how many people are willing to share their slides.

Software to Help You Write

It would be great to have some software that would make the whole process of writing speeches easier. Speech writing takes place in several phases. Initially we scribble down ideas, many of which will be rejected at a later stage. After this we try to create order and start to flesh out the presentation. Finally, we can commit this to a word processed document or enter the text into PowerPoint, Keynote or other presentation software.

Notepad software

Windows and Mac computers are supplied with notepad software and although the formatting options are a little limited, they are fine for getting down your initial thoughts.

Here is Mac's TextEdit. This is a lightweight word processor with just enough tools to allow you to type in your basic text and perform some simple editing. This is absolutely as much as many people need. Most of the bells and whistles of the more complex packages are way more than most of us ever need. There are freeware and shareware notepad programs around for the Mac but with TextEdit available on all Macs there's little need for another.

Windows users have their equivalent in the form of WordPad which is pretty much like TextEdit so use either depending on your machine.

Block out the distractions

While writing, there is always the temptation to use the computer to check email and browse the web, when we are supposed to be writing our speech. Blank out distractions using software which stops you seeing any menus, windows, widgets or gadgets. WriteRoom (Mac) and DarkRoom (PC) are programs that once opened shows you only the cursor and little else. There are no distractions on the screen. This type of software is used mainly by people who write books so they focus solely on the text but there's no reason why it shouldn't be used for speech writing.

Even some word processors are including a "full screen" option to blot out menus and the entire desktop. Apple's software Pages has this feature as standard. So if you are struggling with your writing and need some way of focusing, this could be the solution.

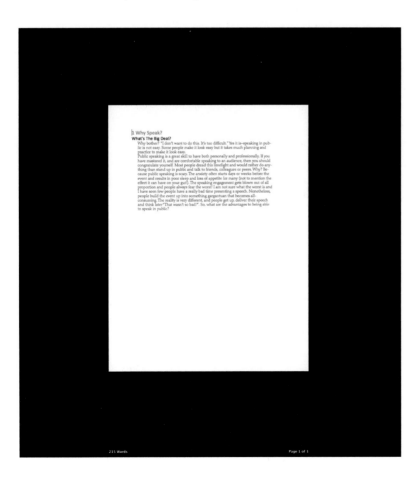

Coping With Anxiety

There are many books and websites dealing with this subject and a few are listed here.

Dorothy Sarnoff is the author of *Never Be Nervous Again* (Mass Market Paperback) in 1987. The book is out of print now but can still be obtained from online booksellers. She clearly understood what it meant to be nervous during presentations and her self-help approach in this small book is excellent. I would recommend you try to get hold of a copy.

Online resources

These include *www.anxietycoach. com*, *www.iampanicked.com*, and *www. trustyguides.com/public-speaking7.html*. You need to decide which one works for you. Search the web yourself and see what looks right for you. The fee-paying services are probably better than the free ones.

If anxiety is impairing your ability to present well and speak in public then these sites should be able to offer help and guidance.

Index

Q

R

S

T

U

V

W

Y

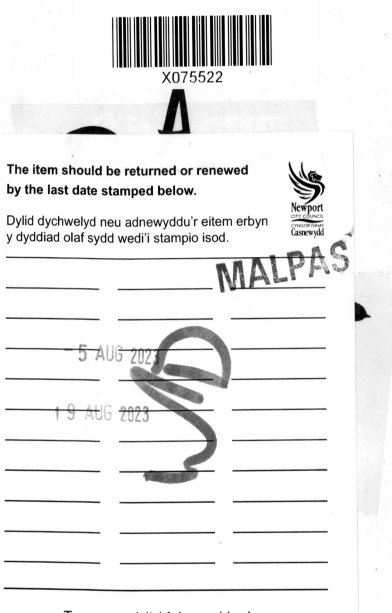

**The item should be returned or renewed
by the last date stamped below.**

Dylid dychwelyd neu adnewyddu'r eitem erbyn
y dyddiad olaf sydd wedi'i stampio isod.

Newport
CITY COUNCIL
CYNGOR DINAS
Casnewydd

To renew visit / Adnewyddwch ar
www.newport.gov.uk/libraries

Also by

HELEN PETERS

LOOK OUT FOR:

A Piglet Called Truffle

A Duckling Called Button

A Sheepdog Called Sky

A Kitten Called Holly

A Lamb Called Lucky

A Goat Called Willow

An Otter Called Pebble

An Owl Called Star

FOR OLDER READERS:

The Secret Hen House Theatre

The Farm Beneath the Water

Evie's Ghost

Anna at War